*Through gates of unparalleled dream,
P'rea Press bids you a thousand welcomes.*

In *The Land of Bad Dreams*, Kyla Ward offers up a rich, eccentric miscellany of dark music, skilfully crafted and strangely wrought. Dream-image or historical horror, vignette or ballad, there is something here to intrigue almost any seeker after the weird.
—Ann Schwader, 2010 Rhysling Award winner for Best Short Poem

Delicious antiquity and delirious archaism mix and mingle in Kyla Ward's verse. With a true poet's sense of language she teases and tantalises the senses—now psychologically acute, now darkly suggestive; here delving into myth and history, there using touches of magic and mystery. Her work draws the reader into a world sometimes eerily threatening, sometimes fascinatingly rococo and Symbolist. In form and fable, Ward is equally at home, and it's not all archaism: from deceptively simple ditties redolent of folk-rhyme and fairytale, to verses delving into skewed manifestations of modernity, Ward demonstrates her mastery and command of sensual language. *The Land of Bad Dreams* is a haunting collection. It deserves a place alongside the works of Angela Carter, Joyce Carol Oates, Tanith Lee, Mirra Lokhvitskaya, and Leonora Carrington, but Ward's voice is all her own.
—Leigh Blackmore, President, Australian Horror Writers Association

Nocturnal, toothy, grisly and witty . . . a carnival of life's cruel and grotesque side, with much pageant and dark laughter.
—K. J. Bishop, author *The Etched City*

Kyla Ward is a most accomplished poet. *The Land of Bad Dreams* is like some deep plunged mine in the realm of uncharted dream where the reader can take more than his or her share of precious and semi precious stones, not to mention an abundance of silver, gold and even platinum! Her "Herbal Tea" is a sure classic. She calls to this reader's mind the work of Christina Rossetti, especially her peerless "Goblin Market." There are also elements of Walter de la Mare, and Mary Elizabeth Counselman. Ward is a born poet, and knows what she is about in her work, which does, indeed, weave its own potent and subtle magics.
—Michael Fantina, author *Flowers of Nithon*, *This Haunted Sea*

The poetry of Kyla Ward is, much like its author, dark, intricate, and intelligent. A whisper of decadence, a hint of decay, and men and women wrapped in the linen of both.
—Ben Peek, author *Twenty-Six Lies/One Truth, Above/Below*

Kyla Ward's verses will appeal to those interested in the weird tradition of poetry, especially to anyone ever allured by the spells of her elder coven sisters Leah Bodine Drake, Mary Elizabeth Counselman, and Dorothy Quick. In *The Land of Bad Dreams*, one navigates by the lantern light of a goblin moon. It is a strange, dark region of the psyche where demons dwell; where the shadows of myths and ghosts of memories whisper weird charms, hexes and exorcisms.
—Wade German, author, poet

Kyla has real presence "live" as she has too in these poems. She knows the value of the pause, the tease, the ache, the lure of a dream in daylight. There is a transfixing quality and a warning: "mind how you approach."
—Danny Gardner, co-formed the Live Poets Society of North Sydney

Evoking a long poetic tradition in weird fiction, Kyla Ward's *The Land of Bad Dreams* is a collection of thoughtful, atmospheric, melodic dark poetry—replete with the sort of lyricism that drifts into the mind and stays like a recalcitrant guest long afterwards. Here you'll find short lyrical bursts through to tales of epic darkness, offering more than a few moments of exquisite frisson. Though writing in the shadow of Poe and his like, Ward infuses her weird poetry with an integrity all her own. Varied yet effective, traditional yet contemporary, harsh yet graceful, serious yet often touched by a sardonic humour, it is a perfect companion for reading on dark and stormy nights in the flickering light of a candle flame, or down the beach on a sunny day when the spirit can be unexpectedly drawn into contemplation of life's darker currents. Terror and the beauty it can evoke: that's what I expect from poetry like this—and that is what *The Land of Bad Dreams* gave me. This is a collection that should be welcomed by those who love poetry of whatever ilk and may even be embraced by those who don't.
—Robert Hood, author *Immaterial, Creeping in Reptile Flesh*

THE LAND OF BAD DREAMS

THE LAND OF BAD DREAMS

KYLA LEE WARD

Edited by Charles Lovecraft

P'REA PRESS
SYDNEY
2011

KYLA LEE WARD (b. 1969) is an Australian writer, actor and artist devoted to all things dark and beautiful. Her poetry has previously appeared in *Midnight Echo*, *Bloodsongs*, *Abaddon*, and *Gothic.Net*, as well as in live performances. Her novel *Prismatic* (co-authored as "Edwina Grey") won the 2007 Aurealis Award for Best Horror, and her short fiction has appeared in the likes of *Ticonderoga Online*, *Shadowed Realms*, *Borderlands*, and *Macabre: A Journey into Australia's Worst Fears*. She co-edited seven issues of *Tabula Rasa* magazine, and two of her scripts have been performed on stage by the Theatre of Blood repertory company. Her website is Tabula Rasa: http://www.tabula-rasa.info/KylaWard.html

P'rea Press, Sydney Australia. Published September 2011; reprint February 2016.
Poetry and Interview © by Kyla Lee Ward 2011, 2016.
Introduction © by P'rea Press 2011, 2016.
Cover and internal illustrations © by Kyla Lee Ward 2011, 2016.

All rights reserved. Reviewers may quote short passages.
Book designed by David E. Schultz.
Cover designed by David Schembri Studios. Email: dschembristudios@gmail.com
Back cover photo taken by David Carroll.
Publisher's logo created by Charles Lovecraft.
Printed by Lightning Source International.
Set in Goudy Old Style 11 point.

NATIONAL LIBRARY OF AUSTRALIA CATALOGUING-IN-PUBLICATION ENTRY:
Author: Ward, Kyla.
Title: The land of bad dreams / Kyla Lee Ward; Charles Alveric Lovecraft, editor.
ISBN: 9780980462579 (pbk.)
Notes: Includes bibliographical references and index.
Subjects: Gothic poetry (Literary genre).
Australian poetry—21st century.
Other Authors/Contributors:
Lovecraft, Charles.
Dewey Number: 821.008015

To my family

The DEAD leave no token
But DECAY and fade:
Shall our bond be broken
By this new DECAYed?
O lest our lives resume
DeluDEAD and faDEAD,
I declare this volume
To be DEAD DECAY DEAD.

Contents

Introduction	xi
An Interview with Kyla Lee Ward	xv
Part I—Dreams	**1**
The Land of Dreams Gone Bad	3
Night Cars	5
Mary	7
Herbal Tea	9
Deshayes Cradle Song	12
The Torturer's Confession	13
The Flower Maid	16
The Battle Bride	18
The Kite	20
The Soldier's Return	23
Part II—Fables	**27**
The Bat's Boudoir	29
The Cat's Cortège	32
The Rat's Repast	36
Part III—Biohazard	**41**
The Traveller	43
The Grandchild	46
The Sleep of Reason (interrupted)	49
Exorcism	51
The Sculptor	53
Virgins and Martyrs	56
Vespers	59
Day Cars	60

My Guest	62
Hymn	63
The Sleep of Reason (concluded)	65

Part IV—The Feast of Mistrust — 67

i. The Fear	69
ii. The Fare	81
iii. The Feast	93
iv. The Finish	107

Index of Titles — 111

Index of First Lines — 112

Glossary — 113

Selected Bibliography of Kyla Lee Ward — 117

Illustrations

Necropolitan [cover image]	
What an Imagination!	2
Doona Worry!	10
The Battle Bride	19
The Necromancer	21
Little Fangs	28
Into the Mist	42
Scapegoat	48
Bonescape	54
Adoration	58
The Festival	68
The Mistress	80
The Master	94
The Final Offering	106
Day Sleep	109

INTRODUCTION

Dreams and poetry share an innate freedom. Both well from deep within the mind of the poet-dreamer, defying the ordered processes of consciousness. Symbols both universal and personal are allowed free play, producing new possibilities and insights. Travel is possible, and the compression and expansion of time. And, free of barriers as of censors, both may take those privy to the experience into places they might not normally approach. Yet bad dreams can contain valuable truths and dark poetry reveal a beauty inaccessible both to reason and to daylight.

—*Kyla Lee Ward*

The Land of Bad Dreams offers the reader a many faceted view of an extraordinary Australian poet, writer, artist and dramatic performer. In this first collection of Kyla Lee Ward's poetry and prose vignettes we see distilled her uniquely imaginative inner world, her inventiveness with language and poetic forms, and her command of imagery that draws upon past eras and long lost cultures.

The works herein have been selected for their themes of dark fantasy and myth. The volume is arranged in four sections titled Dreams, Fables, Biohazard, and a long poem, "The Feast of Mistrust." The selection covers all periods of Ward's life including the early pieces, "Herbal Tea" and "Night Cars," and works begun in her youth and completed in maturity such as "The Feast of Mistrust." Her own illustrations throughout, a bibliography of her work and an interview with her are revealing of her diverse creative abilities.

On meeting Ward in person, her presence, bearing and the drama of her personality immediately impress and fascinate. She is a consummate performance poet and this tells strongly in her written poetic style. Her poetry is, above all, made for speaking or reading aloud in her own cultured Australian cadence. This characteristic explains much about the idiosyncrasies and strengths of her poetry.

Her poetic works usually tell a story or deliver a message as do most works within an oral tradition whether song, poetry or drama. For example, "The Soldier's Return" tells the tale of a soldier's expectations and revelations on his return home after the wars; "Deshayes Cradle Song" conveys that fate is inexorable, while "Exorcism" posits a rationalist view of the universe. Works such as "The Kite" and "Hymn" take the reader to distant epochs, while in "The Feast of Mistrust" she invokes the entire secret history of a city, building it, as it were, from the ground up.

Ward's vivid imagination has been cultivated through many years of interest in Classical, Egyptian, medieval and gothic aesthetics and culture. Her writing is imbued with atmosphere based on a lifetime of immersion in these other worlds. Even the contemporary setting of "The Sculptor" is nuanced by references to classical Greece and Rome, and by Egyptian images.

Pace and rhythm are central elements in the recitation of Ward's poetry: "I recognize pattern and rhythm, visually, aurally and conceptually." She creates and enhances dramatic effects by shifts between formal and free verse. Formal rhythms, natural language rhythms and the rhythms of free verse are interposed to create pace and add dramatic effect to her performance. For instance, in "The Sculptor" she uses formal verse with eight syllables and both internal and end rhyme for the main structure of the poem, interspersed with free verse to render the ordinary speech of the protagonist. "The Grandchild" presents an inventive mix of lines—mostly rhymed; with lines of different lengths; lines with metrical feet of two or three syllables reminiscent of *amphibrach* and *amphimac* metre; and with unusual line breaks. This variation achieves changes of pace from hesitant or slow to a more even and stronger rendition. The merits of this unconventional style are best perceived when the work is read aloud as in the telling of a story.

However, her adeptness and discipline, in both formal and free verse are well evidenced by extensive writing in each mode. For instance, "Mary," "The Torturer's Confession," "The Flower Maid," "The Battle

Bride," "Day Cars," and "My Guest" are representative of her formal or semi-formal verse; "Night Cars," "The Kite," "Virgins and Martyrs," "Exorcism," and "Hymn" are representative of her free verse.

"The Feast of Mistrust" reveals both her inventiveness and control of formal poetic elements. She has devised and followed a predominantly iambic metrical pattern and unique rhyme scheme for 1,086 lines. This long work has 181 six-line stanzas with the following rhyme scheme: first line has no rhyme; second line rhymes with fourth line; third line has internal rhyme; and fifth line rhymes with sixth line. From "The Feast of Mistrust," Part I, The Fear:

> From eyes and ears and open maws
> that cling to turret stone,
> to carven head and sealing lead
> that holds the dust and bone.
> Ah, slow the church is sinking; it is but the dead who know
> there's inches less in crypt and rat-hole than a year ago.

In her use of language there are interesting shifts between older forms and contemporary idiom. Ward judiciously uses archaic and obscure language in creating and enriching other worldly settings, mood and atmosphere. In several poems she uses Latinisms, such as *"in nomine patris"* ("Virgins and Martyrs"), and *"lex talionis"* ("The Rat's Repast") enhancing settings and moods with detail specific to other times and places. "The Soldier's Return" refers to a "jennet" (a small Spanish horse), connoting medieval Spain. Ward's knowledgeable use of herb-lore also evokes medieval times: "vervain" ("The Soldier's Return"); "hartshorn" ("The Torturer's Confession"); "datura," "must" and "ergot" ("The Feast of Mistrust"). A brief glossary is provided for the reader's convenience.

Yet overall her language and usage is contemporary and widely accessible. Some pieces reflect modern urban vernacular, achieving pace, accessibility of meaning and special effects such as the intimacy of conversation, an aside or other theatrics, for example: "They want it so pure, so sweet and so sad, / and isn't it sick that they want it so bad," from "Virgins and Martyrs."

When considering the influences on Ward's creativity, some names spring to mind instantly such as E. A. Poe. Similarity of their subject matter is obvious but comparisons may also be made between their use of the vernacular. For instance, most of Poe's later poetry is written in the vernacular of the day and he "consciously sought to reproduce the rhythms of conversation" in that work.*

However, there is evidence Ward's reading and ensuing influences have been eclectic. For instance, her use of unconventional "line breaks" ("The Grandchild") suggests familiarity with modern authors who use that device, such as the avid proponent of enjambment, E. E. Cummings (see his poem "old age sticks"). It is not surprising to learn that she was a precocious child, writing poetry before she went to school and continually developing her many arts, dark arts as she calls them, through her youth.

Though culture is a cumulative process and all creators stand on the shoulders of those who went before them, perhaps the compelling interest in Ward's work is the extent to which her appreciation of poetic elements is uniquely manifested in her writing. The shifts of form, style and language express the essential, multi-dimensional, dramatic nature of Ward's creativity. Read any piece and note the many perspectives, spaces and dimensions manifest there; the movement and energy to capture or explore these. There are no static, passive pieces; all are intricately wrought, tensioned, kinetic.

In the northern hemisphere mandrakes grow. Here beneath southern constellations, in our sunburnt land, Australia, strange, potent botanicals twist their roots through stony ground and strain upwards to our harsher, brighter light.

P'rea Press is proud to publish this first collection of Kyla Lee Ward, herself one of those strange, rare species.

—CHARLES LOVECRAFT AND J. T. ROSS

---

* Thomas Ollive Mabbott, ed., from his "Introduction" to *The Collected Works of Edgar Allan Poe: Volume 1, Poems* (Cambridge, MA: Harvard University Press, 1969), xxiv.

An Interview with Kyla Lee Ward

Kyla lives in Sydney with her partner, David, and their cats. She has a Bachelor of Arts, and her curriculum vitae encompasses producing medieval shows for schools; running a Live Action Role-playing company; waitressing in theatre restaurants; media officer for the local chapter of the Greens; programming the horror stream at the 68th World Science Fiction Convention; legal secretary; administrative assistant; advertising sales; writing short stories and novels, role-playing games and magazine articles; stage performances and film work; and artwork.

Sunday, July 24, 2011
Dear Kyla,
You told me last time I visited, about reciting a Keats poem at school when you were young and that the teacher was so impressed she "exported" you to other classrooms to recite there also. To me this suggests an early destiny with poetry.

I was 16 and it was the "Ode to Melancholy." The brief was actually to select a paragraph from one of the texts we had already studied, read it out to the class and discuss it. I knew we were scheduled to study Keats that year and had already read substantially from a little volume that belonged to my grandfather—a volume I still cherish today. I simply thought that doing this would be more interesting, and "Ode to Melancholy" was my favourite.

What happened then, how many class rooms did you recite "Melancholy" in that time?

I think it was only one: the other "A" stream class who would also be studying Keats.

Did anyone laugh?

Not at the time, but two of my friends shot a video parodying my performance. Yeah, my friends were like that. And I was inured from being laughed at by that point, oh well and truly.

How old were you when you first recited verse?

This is a tough one. Because, well, the fact is I was *writing* verse at age 4. A few years later, my second-grade teacher was so impressed by the poem I wrote describing fireworks that she made it the basis of a class project. If you don't believe me, I can show you the damn thing. I would imagine that I began reciting verse concurrently to these developments.

What prompted it?

Verse simply seems to be how my mind works. I recognise pattern and rhythm—visually, aurally and conceptually. When I was that young, I didn't have to try and memorise poetry, I just did. It's not something I can easily bring onto the conscious plane; for instance, I failed at all my efforts to study music. The pace of a poem is all but physical to me.

Was it nursery rhymes in primary school, or on television?

Ah now, this I can answer. It was my mother reading to me from a large volume of classic poems for children. I remember being very fond of "Lochinvar" by Sir Walter Scott and all of T. S. Eliot's *Old Possum's Book of Practical Cats* . . . They may indeed be the first things I remember actually reciting.

How does it make you feel when you read poetry aloud?

Sometimes poetry is meant to be read aloud; the words contain the performance. Some poems contain *movement*; they must be enacted or even danced. You can waltz to Poe's "Ulalume," and "The War-Song of Dinas Vawr" by Thomas Love Peacock must be beaten out with a fist. I feel words like some people feel music.

You exude an actor's poise and confidence when you recite in front of an audience—did you do any formal training for this level of expertise?

I commenced formal drama tuition with Australian actress and speech coach Judy Burgess, at age 12. I remained in various incarnations of the Australian Children's Theatre School (ACTS) until I was 17, playing roles such as Queen Titania in *A Midsummer Night's Dream*.

Did you perform in any plays or other productions at school?

In Primary School, I wrote and directed plays! Not that I'm making any claim for the literary merit of *The Mice in the Throne Room*, but even before joining ACTS, that was the kind of thing I did.

Have you been on the stage as an adult?

There were intermittent outings, such as my attempt to establish a mask troupe in 1998 (that managed one performance at a banquet given by the Medieval and Renaissance Society, before imploding spectacularly), the usual run of Tropfest entries and Short & Sweet, and poetical performances in association with Pagans in the Pub and *Abaddon*, up until 2009, when I won a place in the newly-formed Theatre of Blood repertory company. This troupe is devoted to staging contemporary and classic works of the Grand Guignol, the French theatre of the macabre. I have played such roles as the Curator in *The Guillotine*, Annie in *The Torture Garden*, and Gatea Criollo in my own *Chocolate Curses*.

Do you have a sense that you are carrying on the oral tradition?

Oh now, this is hard to quantify, as I can't really claim to have inherited one, despite the Welsh ancestry! But going on the evidence of my *other* writings, I have to say I *believe* in one. The *recitator* (Latin), who keeps alive the great epics containing the history and law of the people, plays a core role in my (unpublished) fantasy novel *Secret Paths*. I do truly believe that we know ourselves and the world through stories; not so much the ones we read as the ones we repeat.

What does poetry mean to you personally?

Some ideas must be articulated in rhyme. Some must be written in free verse. Some are suitable for short stories or scripts; some grandiose complexities mean novels. Don't ask me to explain how the choice is made, because it's not a choice.

On poetry specifically, I have recourse to a quote from Herodotus, the Grecian chronicler who wrote in the 5th century BCE: "I came myself as a herald from lovely Salamis, but with song on my lips instead of common speech." Salamis is an island off the coast of Greece that was historically claimed by both Athens and Megara. In the 6th century, the rulers of Athens had become so weary of the ongoing dispute they passed a law forbidding the people to discuss it. By reciting a poem of his own composition in the marketplace, Solon both side-stepped the law and persuaded them to wage war. Poetry is that which lies above and beyond common speech, expressing things that cannot otherwise be said and kindling the mind as nothing else will.

What prompted "The Feast of Mistrust"—a very interesting and coiling piece of work?

Okay, the grisly truth is that parts of this piece—not many, but some lines—date from Christmas Day 1986. Unable to cope with the festive family luncheon a moment longer, I ran outside, opened my notebook and started writing (yes, of course I had a notebook and pen with me—why do you ask?) Among those initial scrawls were the words, "the feast of mistrust." That's all I'm saying about *that*.

Completing the work was an extremely long and convoluted process: the protagonists all arrived over a space of years and both Lady Webbe and Doctor Wulf have had other homes. But this is their real story. The project lay fallow for years at a time, but I could never abandon it. In some way I can't say it in anything less than 1,086 lines, it is too important.

Do you have a favourite poem in the collection?

Oh dear. Well, as I said in my interview in *Eye of Fire*, I am extremely fond of "Mary," the poem that arrived full and complete in a dream, and is fun to recite to Goth friends while trawling cemeteries late at night. But how could I slight "Herbal Tea," that distilled my teenage obsession with herbs and herbals, and to be absolutely honest, the movie *Labyrinth*? What about "The Traveller," that began as an incantation during my trips to and from university, the meaning evolving as time went by? Fair to say they have all been my favourite at some point or another!

Which poems mean the most to you?

Oh dear, dear. Well, I should imagine the reader would be able to narrow it down. I've given them my autobiography in verse, after all! Let me just say that I do not invoke the dark powers lightly or without reason.

What do you think, expect, or want readers should get from your work?

Oh dear, dear, dear! They will get whatever they take. I have simply attempted to open up a conceptual space that perhaps did not exist for them before.

Siren. And with that she leaves us at the mercy of her song. Her poems are just round the bend of the page . . .

—Charles (Danny) Lovecraft
P'rea Press

Part I
Dreams

What an Imagination!

The Land of Dreams Gone Bad

The parties have all run on too long
and the girl who hid too well
peers from the cracks, waiting for the game to end.
Here, abrasive twilight lingers on
a crust of wrap and shell
iced with cold wax, as scavengers descend.
Where have the girls and boys all gone?
To the car park and hotel
beside the tracks: there's nothing left to pretend
in the land of dreams gone bad.

Here, Cinderella cuts her foot,
the bad wolf wears a hood
and even witches die in the sights of a gun.
The executive have their input
and the story will look good
with colour pictures on the news at one.
Her parents wait amongst the soot
for her to appear as she should.
Her conscience twitches. But nothing can be done
in the land of dreams gone bad.

There was a prince; at least, she thought
it was his face she saw
within the scrying mirror where all things pass.
And even though it came to naught
she felt what she could; or
does he still lie trapped in a coffin of glass?
Perhaps a hundred years will sort
him out; one thing is sure,
a kiss won't pry him loose. Still, princes are sparse
in the land of dreams gone bad.

The palace should be somewhere near:
once, within the mirror she
saw masquers running light across the snow.
Through secret door, down the passage drear,
and in the court of night the
candles burn unending; for there is no
birthday there, no accreted year,
only everlasting beauty
and strength. But none will show her how to go
in the land of dreams gone bad.

It's late; surely they're calling now
or do only crows hover
harshly inviting her to the feast begun?
If she emerged with courtly bow
and wrapping paper over
her clothes, the sight might be a welcome one.
Dare she move, through broken gifts, how
painfully from cover,
into last light? Surely, by now, she has won
in the land of dreams gone bad.

Night Cars

When sleep wraps the house in a blanket of wool
and dulls the rooms in an opaque mist,
when your eyes peer out of the marshes of sleep,
merging your flesh with the fester below,
then you may hear the night cars.

Sleek, hungry as sharks,
they cruise the streets seeming
to stare with their empty seats.
Slowly, smoothly, serried they circle,
to focus on
could it be
you?

When you wake in the night for no reason,
grope for the blanket and hide
in the pit of your mind,
in the pit of your gut,
in the festering darkness below,
muffle your ears to the sound of the night cars.

They roar like a sea wave,
foam hissing down the deserted street.
A gale in the tree-tops thunders
and dies to
a whisper.
Hide.

You may see their headlights in arcs on the ceiling,
circling patterns but
hide.
Hide.

Do not succumb.
For go to see the night cars
and they will hunt you.
They will find you.
And when morning comes all there will be
are rags of skin and scattered clumps of
hair at the
side of the
road.

Mary

Come into the graveyard, Mary,
hinderance of thorns defying.
Eyes that still can see are chary,
ears unstopped by clay are prying.
Through the trees like witches dancing,
deep into the twilight's bruising,
between their black fingers lancing
stones in shadow shape are losing.
Wind a-running through the grasses
makes the crow's head leap,
and as the rotting wreaths it passes,
sings itself to sleep.

Come into the graveyard, Mary,
past there the cold iron fencing.
Here no kin is watching wary,
no friend here goodwill pretensing.
Past the doors that need not open
for their tenants always smiling.
Through the twisted branches groping
peer the clouds' dull eyes, beguiling.
Those beneath us deeply ground
the pathway that before us lies.
Step and down and turn around
and look me in the eyes.

Come into the graveyard, Mary,
E'en as sudden fear restrains.
Breathe the dust so deep and lairy,
feel the blood thin in your veins.
I am fire, I am lightness
and the roaring water's life

and now held here in the darkness,
you will always be my wife.
Flesh to mine and heart be numb,
for fingers cold, my dear,
entwined do not unclasp. Now come,
and know we shall lie here.

HERBAL TEA

Goblins sleep in the roots of herbs,
where cats' eyes peep in the roots of herbs.
Intricacies of tiny limbs,
of crawling, gnarled and hidden things.
Secret juices, fragrant life,
a monkshood and an iron knife
cross uneasy over the fey
rustles from the dim-dawned day.
Leathern books and old proverbs,
shadows creep in the roots of herbs.

Goblins hide in the roots of herbs,
careless bride in the roots of herbs,
garland-winding lost her way
forever; taken, here she lay.
Imprisoned, mingled, roots her grief,
her veil became the scented leaf
and in the earth the unkissed wife
found no grave but stranger life.
She waits by overgrown kerbs.
Secrets sighed in the roots of herbs.

Goblins lurk in the roots of herbs,
uncanny work in the roots of herbs.
Precious powers hold that stem,
strange aches of flesh are linked to them.
Feathered shard of root so round,
drawing deep to underground.
Kitchen windows, walls of brick,

Doona Worry!

in pavement cracks the hint will stick.
From castles to decayed suburbs;
oh, never shirk the roots of herbs.

Goblins watch in the roots of herbs,
for lore will cost in the roots of herbs.
Fear to enter such a maze
where distilled ichors cure or craze.
Seductive leaves their fragrance waft,
a half-seen hand, a hidden laugh,
and when such things are known to me,
what should I drink but herbal tea?
A toast! To all that peace disturbs,
and children lost in the roots of herbs.

Deshayes Cradle Song

What does it take to kill a mouse?
It takes a cat to kill a mouse.
It takes a cat to kill a mouse
and catch him in his house,
so every little mouse
must work and play not knowing when his cat will come.

What does it take to kill a cat?
It takes a dog to kill a cat.
It takes a dog to kill a cat
and eat him nice and fat,
so every pretty cat
must work and play not knowing when his dog will come.

What does it take to kill a dog?
It takes a bull to kill a dog.
It takes a bull to kill a dog
and toss him on the nog,
so every gallant dog
must work and play not knowing when his bull will come.

What does it take to kill a bull?
It takes a man to kill a bull.
It takes a man to kill a bull
and sure he is no fool,
so every clever bull
must work and play not knowing when his man will come.

What does it take to kill a man?
It takes a death to kill a man.
It takes a death to kill a man,
so each clever or gallant,
or pretty little man
must work and play not knowing when his death may come.

The Torturer's Confession

I am a master of exacting craft.
Be certain, Sir, you are in worthy hands.
My talents were uncovered by the draft
and now I find myself in some demand.
Great lords demand, I know, but do not fret:
we left him far above. He doesn't care
to watch my work and this is better yet,
for he would surely be amazed to hear
my craft makes no demands. It merely asks.
How looked the sky, Sir? Will there be more rain?
How goes the harvest and your daily tasks?
Come walk with me through my humble domain!

Ah yes, I know what draws your roving eye.
None can ignore her; here, 'tis she that rules,
but play the game, give her excuse to try.
Come look at these, such exquisite tools
as scarce admit a finger. Turn the screw
and they grow smaller than you would suppose.
I'm fond of such machines, come close and you
will see this suits the tongue and this the nose.
See this sleek bulb, so cunningly wrought
it seems to be a lady's missing gawd?
But twist the knob, a lily blossoms forth
each petal edged and rigid as a sword.
This chamber's deep, the river very near
and stone transmits a dankness to the air;
perhaps that's why you shake. Come over here,
I keep a fire alight beside this chair.
But give the chair a glance before you sit.
Such straps and braces, much as surgeons use

to the same purpose: to ensure the fit.
But note the holes enable me to choose
as gardener, where this rare bulb to lay!
If you prefer to keep your stance, well then;
this boot will wear as well as iron may.
A little large, but it fits snugly when
the gap about is filled with burning coals.
Care not to stand? Then there are ways to hang
suspended by the seven native holes
that will not kill, although it cost a pang.

But I've been teasing. If you'll turn around?
My lady may appear reserved and straight
with her cold breast by chain and leather bound,
but I dare say she's not inviolate!
For others have lain down with her before.
She makes men scream, the pretty, wanton wretch!
She'll clasp you tight, as one she does adore,
take your full measure, then begin to stretch.
So like a woman! Whatever man might do,
she would have faster, harder, longer, more!
Till breaks your back and snaps your tendon through.
Oh, she will leave you satisfied, be sure.
Why, you look faint! A drop of aquavit?
A sniff of hartshorn? Or the sting of salt?
All proven to retrieve a person's wit.
Choose now, to sit, stand, lie, ascend the vault –
confess? You'd flee this worthy battlefield
with lance unbroke and blade not even drawn?
Have courage, Sir! You cannot think to yield
arriving here so near unto the dawn.
Think on your honour: think on silent death.
Is not this mortal life a vale of tears?
All that I have assailed you with is breath.
All that I have assaulted are your ears.

* * *

I am a master: all here know it well.
Whilst still a child I cut the heads off fowl
and watched the bodies run until they fell.
Now I do counsel both the crown and cowl.
I have a seat reserved for me in church,
a house they call mine, a wife much the same.
The rivals for my secret fiercely search,
not knowing that my secret is my shame.
That I succeed the best wherein I fail
to use the skills that were so painfully won
as surgeon following the army's trail.
A master, whose own craft has him undone.
How long since these tools were to purpose put?
Or my hands felt that oh, most holy thrill
of weighing every separate cut
between persuasion and the final kill?
Every day I fear those gifts will flee;
escape me much like my ungrateful charge.
And is this how God seeks to punish me
or in this room does Satan loom so large?
Here now, alone, I make tally precise
of all my tricks; my hearth, my chair and bed,
and fancy it's my finger in the vice.
My foot. My eye. My anus, tongue or head.
Mine other hand is resting on the screw.
How would it feel? What would I ask of me?
And how far could I go before I knew
that I might meet the axe in honesty?

THE FLOWER MAID

A maiden dwelt within this glade,
a queen in all but name.
Her gleaming hair,
like sunbeams fair,
put earthly gold to shame.

Her eyes were as the clearest sky
framed by the whitest thorn,
and if their role
reflects the soul,
she was pure as Spring morn.

By day she wore a dress of brown,
by dusk a cloak of blue.
But when first sun,
true silver spun,
she bathed herself in dew.

As each new dawn decked tree and pool
with fringe of liquid pearls,
downing her smock,
in linen frock,
she loosed her golden curls.

A trembling branch of jasmine sweet
would kiss her brow and neck.
And next she chose
the spangled rose,
her soft cheek to bedeck.

Her hands sought the magnolia
to gain a perfume rare,
while fresh sunbeams'
caressing streams
would place a diamond there.

A faerie vision then she seemed,
straying to mortal sight,
the dew on stems
and petals her gems,
and rayed about with light.

So fair she was that toiling day
felt shamed taking its due,
and thus one morn
the maid was gone,
had faded with the dew!

But though the night still haunts the trees,
at lightest kiss of sun,
adrift of mist
in stately bliss,
the maiden comes! She comes!

Where blossom rising on the bough
a living church-glass wrought,
an elvan sprite
of purest light,
a queen of fragrant court!

THE BATTLE BRIDE

As proudly sound the martial drums,
the bride in purple gown she comes.
Stands the groom in a warrior's garb,
with sword and spear of silver barb.
He sips the wine that's touched her lips,
as gold onto her finger slips;
tastes her mouth through scarlet lace,
then gazes on his consort's face.
Skips his heart and halts his breath,
he stares into the eyes of Death!
Too late sees that which clasps his own,
gold glimmering on a hand of bone.
No youthful maid but withered wight,
the skin of Death is flaking white.
Unbreakable the ring-sealed troth,
his lips bleed from her jagged mouth!
In horror strives to break the clasp,
but finds himself in an iron grasp.
The chill strikes to his very bone,
she saps his strength to make her own.
No venture found, no honoured role,
but into darkness sinks his soul.
Where is the glory in a tomb?
And now the drums are drums of doom.

The Battle Bride

The Kite

She goes home tonight.
By day she mourns like a wet nurse,
giving her tears to those not her own.
She walks in procession through the necropolis,
beating her breast and tearing her hair;
good figure, long hair and she never stints.
The troupe leader favours her. She always
shares the funeral meal and coin.
But tonight, as torches cluster at the gate
like the bright clouds cluster in the west, she goes home.
Not to the city of the living,
but back into the silent clutter of tombs.
This place is old. The watchmen keep
to the paved roads and crypts with names.
But centuries pass as she walks uphill,
treading shards of sculpture, fragments of stone
and bronze. No lights here, no offerings;
such things attract worse than dogs.
That's why she broke the seals after the funeral,
to keep him safe. She remembers that day:
yellow is the colour of funerals,
of sunlight, disease and the flesh of women.
Now the sky is indigo and wind creeps chill
through a door that she opened, inch by inch,
to a crypt whose first owner had been erased,

The kite is connected symbolically to the sacred myth of Isis and Osiris. Thus, from a very early period in Ancient Egypt, the word *djert* referred both to professional mourners and the bird of prey. The funeral ritual and the reuse of an ancient tomb reflect conditions in the Theban necropolis at the end of the New Kingdom.

The Necromancer

barely large enough to contain his outer shell.
Not a good likeness: no likeness at all.
The symbol of a man. They placed it here
and left him. It took her weeks to work the lid aside.
Now her hands sink into linen ripped asunder.
A robber, seeing this, will dig no more,
but he still lies just as he did
when the priest anointed the eyes and mouth
of his mask. A likeness there;
the faintest identity in red and black.
Then they drew the shroud across.
No house since then, no name; for there was
no child and his brother didn't want her.
She did not want him. She was a child herself
when they married. But she knew love.
Red is for the flesh of men. Through bandages,
at last she touches; her feet slip through the crack.
Sinking through shrouds and shawls, the scent
of spices replaced by resin.
Her body measures his.
Her hand explores the coldness of his chest.
Cheek to a shoulder hard and slick
as a carved pillow. Deep in the linen of their bed
she rests. Beside him she can sleep.

The Soldier's Return

The ride was hard and howling dark
had bitten me through to the bone,
but how could I begrudge its mark
now every hillock spoke of home?

When lanterns scattered like bright seed
across black fields inscribed a sign –
the only writ I cared to read!
Oh what a welcome would be mine!

Returning I to kith and kin
with honour and a soldier's pay,
and tales of valour; to begin
the life I might have thrown away.

Returning I a broidered scarf
so softly laid across my hands
by one whose sorrow still could laugh
with eyes that haunted other lands.

And as the moon surpassed the cloud,
shedding a pale and pure light,
I thought how sweetly she had vowed
to wait and watch for me by night.

I led my jennet through the slick
and sighing shade within the trees.
I felt the brush and scatter quick
of things unseen about my knees.

I seemed enspelled to make no sound:
I'm not one to imagine bane,

but now I felt unease confound
my joy as smoke the moon might stain.

So to a secret, sheltered dell,
of frosted grass and blackened fern,
that in our childhood we knew well
and once of age we did not spurn.

Then from the black rose silver-white:
my love, my love was standing there
and though she looked as angel might
I saw the vervain in her hair.

On Sunday mornings, piously,
I'd seen her kneel before the cross,
had heard her praised for modesty
and tending well her father's house.

Had kissed her lips and held her near,
but never gone beyond those bounds.
How could it be that I saw here
the signs that sorcery surrounds?

The dagger and the smoking brands,
the cockerel with broken crest,
the bloody basin in her hands,
the star encircled on her breast.

The wind shook both the low and tall,
as though the sky had royal tides
and here came madness, drowning all
my horror and my fear besides!

There could be thunder passing through,
or did I hear the martial drum
I left behind? All that I knew
was if she beckoned, I must come.

But on the blood her gaze was set,
a dreadful working to begin,
and as the fumes did twist and fret
I vow I saw myself within.

My image rode amidst the haze
of flame consuming croft and town,
I saw me set the rooves ablaze
and cut the fleeing people down.

I saw me seize the sacral gold,
a fearful priest wasting his breath.
The boy whose cowardice I told,
making him seek a needless death.

The children whose last crust I seized
and other gallant deeds I did;
the men I'd slaughtered on their knees,
the women I had roughly rid.

I saw her see all that I was
and thought that I could leave behind.
No matter whose the crown or cause,
here I would no redemption find.

And did she pass? For she was gone
perhaps into the tinctured air,
perhaps in shape of foal or fawn
that passed and left me standing there.

And so, my love, we wander yet,
each with our secret to repine.
How can we our course homeward set
now I know yours and you know mine?

Part II
Fables

Little Fangs

The Bat's Boudoir

Observe Madame Chiroptera, flitting from dresser to armoire and back once more to her cavernous bed. Observe, though this chamber within chambers is secluded from every breath of outside air, and there is no light save the phosphorescent face of the clock. Tapering fingers brush atomiser and jar, pluck bead and comb. She knows the location of the least pin. She knows the angle of the footstool to the chair, the curves of the ewer and basin. She knows the route, with its windings and turnings, its many confusing twists, which leads to the door outside. But that can, must wait until the incandescence of the world is tempered by night.

In the meantime, she makes her preparations. She swathes herself in silk and bone, a garment both armour and allure. Silver drops ornament her exquisite ears. Only her eyes are left unadorned. She cares for scent, does our Madame, and much for sound, but her eyes sense only the presence and absence of light. She wears those deep and clouded pools like a mask.

And so prepared she makes her way, at the appointed hour, through the secret ways of her house. There are in these chambers many locked chests and, strange to say, thickets of canes, groves of dinner jackets, and shoals of cigarette cases and watches lying in the dark. By the door, with its granite lintel, hang cloaks of every kind. But the one that envelops her when she steps outside is always the finest grey leather.

There is a space of alleys, of further twists and turns, and then she is among them. Upon the streets, as the gas lamps bloom against the evening sky, crowd the mayfly ladies and their magnificent moths. They trail gauzy veils and coils of gold wire spring from their brows, studded with topaz and aquamarine. Their fine whiskers quiver over velvet lapels, each supernally gorgeous, seducing the very light that draws them out to dance in the mild air. Yet she passes in grey, her presence unremarked. By the sequence of lights, she picks a path to le Café Naturel. Here she sings.

A noted singer, our Madame Chiroptera, amongst a certain class. Let those who will, speak of The Nightingale, or that sultry performer, La Cicada. Madame Chiroptera is for the subtle, who can see a song passing through the smoke and feel it through the stem of a wineglass. The cloak parts and they see the pulsing of her constrained breast, the tiny jewels of her nails. And as she sings the café and all its accoutrements become real to her; each lamp, each table, each patron in their place. As she sings, she finds her prey. She seeks softness, sweetness, a tender youth in rich dress, and pitches her voice to him. She bends on him those wide, blind eyes and seems to beg for succour, for in this city all predators must go disguised, and the victim provides the tempo to the hunt. Velvet crosses her path, with a faint aroma of orchids. He is tall, this one, taller than she usually dares but so willowy, wavering there on the edge of her perception. He has fixed upon her, that is certain.

When she leaves the café he follows hesitantly, weaving back and forth in her wake. There is barely a rustle of coat, which she feigns not to hear, drawing him down through the alleys until, beneath a lone lantern, she turns. Her lips part, but not so wide as to reveal her teeth. Most need no further encouragement, but still this one hangs back, breath coming shortly. She must take the lead, expressing fear for his safety this deep in the maze and insisting she shelter him. They do not quite touch, she fluttering lightly and he still weaving around her, as they enter her lair.

In the dark she takes his sleeve to guide him past her hoard. This close, his scent is strong and she feels his grace, how smoothly he glides beside her. She will drain him first and set his husk to crumble in one of her many rooms. She will spend his money; then, if his belongings are unmarked, pawn them as she needs. Whispering softly, she draws him across the carpet of dust and fur and old lovers, into that deep chamber where the clock remains the only light, and everything is ready. Fingers brush velvet, leather unfurls and they coil around each other, pressing tight.

His embrace is crushing; breath hissing into her face. She pulls back and is denied; they stumble, and the footstool topples. Nails scrape through velvet to reveal a cold roughness. No longer the shape of a sweet, young morsel but a living fetter, tightening about her with every beat of her heart. The bones of her corset begin to snap, but she cannot break free. How can this be? She who hunts without eyes, deceived by perfume and a shed skin? She feels his tongue curl against her cheek.

So that tongue she bites! As her fangs pierce the delicate organ, the coils around her spasm, yet she holds. Madame Chiroptera knows how to hold. He thrashes, battering dresser and drawer, grip squeezing and loosening, and she finds the space to flap! A terrible shudder runs through him from tip to tail, and she is free, beating and raking, clawing her way to the furthermost niche in the uppermost arch of her bed.

And so we must leave them, bat screeching from the roof, snake writhing about on the floor. Both have been surprised in their night's adventures, and while the snake cannot see in the dark, the bat cannot fix on his ever-moving form, turning her bower into chaos. It may be they will have words to share, once they recover their dignity. For if there is one thing on which all predators of the city agree, it is that prey makes for boring conversation.

The Cat's Cortège

See the Mademoiselles Felis approach along the crowded hall; young, slim and neat, in black coats and white gloves, their huge eyes glancing this way and that.

"Too crowded," hisses Mignon.

"With strangers," spits Belle.

"I don't like it!"

"Why'd Papa have to go and die?"

No answer from the casket: the protruding tips of white whiskers give not the slightest quiver. His daughters make their obsequies, aware of the purr of voices all around.

"What are they saying?" whispers Mignon. Belle supplies the truth they both know.

"That Mama will have to marry Uncle Thomas."

Madame Felis is as sleek as her daughters in mourning and in danger herself of being buried by her escort. For Uncle Thomas is huge. A white ruff tops a mound of striped belly, overlooked by yellowish eyes. A quirk of hair makes a crooked M of his forehead as he smiles.

"Hello, my kits." Hungry, that smile, the teeth long and sharp. His breath smells of old meat.

"Hello Uncle."

"How pretty you look today. 'Tis a shame poor Tim cannot see."

"Papa was always watching us." Mignon gazes winningly, but as his big paw moves towards her, she bats it away. Mama pounces.

"What kind of behaviour is this? Show respect to your Uncle, else who knows what may become of us!"

"I assure you," he rumbles, "all you ladies are under my protection." But the glance Mama gives him is fearful.

"Run along now," she says, "the hearse will be here soon and then we shall ride through the streets."

"I don't like it," mews Mignon, as they slip away past tippets and tails.

"Don't like *him*," yowls Belle.

Compromised by death, the house is still their territory. They know its doorways and detours, its corners and crannies, each place where they may disappear. The front stairs offer a speedy escape and there they sit and watch the movement below with narrowed eyes.

"What now?" says Mignon.

"We could stalk the housekeeper."

"Or tease Canary."

"We should have treats."

This, once stated, is obvious, but their route is far from clear. To reach the kitchen without crossing the hall, they can only take the stairs from Papa's chamber. This has always been forbidden on pain of horrors Mama would not describe, but which seemed connected to the proximity of platters and knives. Of course, that was when Papa was in a position to notice.

The door swings open at Mignon's tap. Beyond, all is quiet and still, in the disarray of his final night. Hunger forgotten, the girls explore slowly. The top of the dresser is theirs now, with its foreign array of brushes and medicaments. The depths of the wardrobe, with its tumble of collars, waistcoats and socks. The high reaches of the bed are soft and yielding.

"What's this then? My two kits!"

Mignon leaps to the floor: Belle looks to the door. But it is the panel concealing the stairs that has opened and Uncle Thomas who emerges, squeezing his bulk through an opening that seems to be simply too small. He has been to the kitchen, for there are crumbs down his front and droplets cling to his moustache.

"What do you here, today of all days?"

"We're playing."

"Just playing."

The M twists as that yellow gaze gathers the sisters together. Uncle Thomas, it seems, is still hungry. "Well, that's fine by me. Funerals can be so dull. I would like to play with you, my kits. If we don't tell your Mama, would that be alright?"

Eyes like absinthe moons regard him, paired as a drunk might see them. Uncle Thomas is still thirsty. He peers past them, to check that the door is shut. The girls exchange glances.

"Yes, we want to play," purrs Mignon.

"We want to play hide and seek," chirps Belle.

Uncle Thomas smiles. "Indeed my kits, that's a fine game."

"There's no one else up here," pouts Mignon, "no one will know."

"The front door is home," Belle warns, "so you must catch us before we can reach it."

"I think I can do that, my kits. Yes, I can do that."

Madame Felis curls alone in the undertaker's carriage. Canary has been sent to find the absent, but the procession cannot be held for long. Her relations and neighbours have already taken their places in the long train; how elegant they are, these drawing-room queens, and each the mistress of her own small world! Dark brotherhoods attend them, and what a world of meaning lies in each glance and gesture, degrees of approach and retreat. What terrible deals are made each day and night behind the façade of this genteel street.

The sombre plumes of Rook & Raven wave in the windows; the cortège must be off. With only a moment's hesitation, she waves and the whole elaborate mechanism of the funeral creaks into motion. The hearse's suspension groans, the wheels turning heavily under the weight, it seems, of lilies.

It is at that moment, as the hearse approaches the narrow alley beside the house, that the servant's door bursts open and two lithe figures dart out, pursued by one grosser, in an unpardonable state of undress. The black and white sprites pause one instant before hurling themselves beneath the carriage: their pursuer plunges after with a snarl and not so much as a sidelong glance. Madame Felis screams. The birds flap and horses rear but not before the wheels of the hearse have passed twice over the corpulence of Uncle Thomas.

"We were playing," says Mignon, as the jackals and vultures descend.
"Just playing," echoes Belle.
"Like we used to do with Papa."
"Just the same, when he wanted to play with us."
"Except we took him up onto the roof."
"He should have landed on his feet!"

To which there is little Madame Felis can say. For although hunting is the way of the city, the line twixt predator and prey is thin for those who are born with teeth.

The Rat's Repast

Observe Monsieur Murine, for he is a gourmet of unusual kind. Shabby in his furs, no gloves upon his hands, he nonetheless infiltrates the best houses, the finest dinners. Black truffle out of season? Port older than the clock tower? Such candies as would tempt the Mandarin Duck? Speak to Murine. He knows all the secrets of the city's larders and cellars, can access the most exclusive. A bribe here, a favour there: perhaps a dip into the underworld. For a fee plus expenses, any craving may be satisfied. He does not deal in weapons, in papers or jewels but strictly the ephemera of appetite.

Still, the Hound gives him trouble. Guardian of the public peace, which he himself disturbs with the alarum of the chase, the Hound cuts an impressive figure. The great find him honourable, but those who run the alleys and sewers see his teeth. He sports with the small and harmless, and cornered, all Murine can do is twitch.

"But Captain, I do no wrong! See? These are but the fruits of prickly pear, chestnut honey and a fine camembert obtained for the Marquesa Pigeon—"

"Who if she does exist is a fool. You'll have to do better, vermin!"

"Better than camembert? Ah, Roquefort aged in the caves of Combalou!"

"I'll have no such rubbish! The dish I crave is composed of the tenderest parts of fresh, young hares; such leverets as no other has touched. Their lips and tongues, their breasts and thighs, all well liquored. Find me that and perhaps I will forget my suspicions."

"I fear you are mistaken," Murine squeaks. "I do not deal in such—"

"You do now, else the watch is on your tail! At the Kennel, by midnight!"

The trap thus set is obvious. Such procurement is indeed illegal and the Hound will have him by tail and throat. But fail and not only his freedom will be lost. A single bark could bar his access to the tables of the great.

One crimson fruit and the crumbs of the camembert, these are his comfort. He does not begrudge his clients the bulk of the dish: on the contrary, he thinks they limit themselves most unwisely. Through their unwitting agency, he experiences sensations unrivalled, combinations unheard of, flavour constantly succeeding to flavour. To live any other way is unthinkable, yet how may he protect himself with the friendship of butlers and the resources of pantries? He knows the chef at the Kennel, it's true, and their cellarer; the maids that wash their linen and scrub their floors. All are vermin to the Hound.

The more Murine considers, the more it seems he has not only the solution in hand, but a duty. A sacred trust to once see his fellows fed. A favour here, a bribe there; indeed, he must descend to the underworld this day! Many efforts combine to make a meal, but only he and he alone can set this most *recherché* of menus.

The Kennel may not be the most exclusive of clubs, but its baths equal those anywhere. The Hound reposes in steaming water and contemplation of the pleasures to come. Clove and orange mask the stench of wet hair and also the tang of spirits. They have mingled with his bath from the start but the next top-up tinges the water. Such luxury to bathe in the finest fortified wine! Yet he is oblivious. Chin sinks heavily upon chest and limbs relax. So relaxed those limbs, so hot the water; deeper the colour now and flowing darker, thicker as the furnaces are stoked.

At the appointed hour, Murine leads a procession to the side door. They are expected: the room is prepared and service ready to commence to table. All that lacks is their host.

Delicately, Murine explains the meal is for the ladies. Doubtless the Hound will join them in due course. Behind him, bright eyes peep between tippets and muffs, excited by the night and the adventure. Or is it by the prospect of food? Are they not a little skinny, these creatures with their long fingers and twitching noses? Is not that one a trifle whiskery? Even when ensconced in the Kennel's upholstered chairs with glasses of sherry, they do not doff their costume, as Murine explains that the first dish is a delicacy known as black blood soup.

Black indeed, it simmers in the Kennel's fluted bowls, exhaling the savour of port. But blood? The first to dare pronounces it delicious. Soon all are slurping with glee.

"Next, the chef is pleased to offer an entree of steamed sweetbreads, accompanied by a sparkling wine."

"So this is how they do at those fancy dinners?" says the whiskery one, who also seems somewhat older than specified.

"Indeed it is, my mouse. Permit me to refill your glass."

For the remove, a game ragout involving many parts of the beast. The diners' enthusiasm wavers not as wine kindles ears and noses.

"Where is the Captain, do you suppose?" asks one gone entirely pink. Murine waves grandly.

"If his duties have cost us his company, let us console ourselves with the sweet. Marrow pudding, accompanied by gelatin and a delightful marsala."

"We shouldn't have done this!" bursts from Pink. "If the dogs recognise us, we're—"

"Keep your voice down!" Whiskers wields her spoon prohibitively. "How *else* would they recognise us?"

"At least you've the hole he expects!"

"I beg you not to trouble yourselves!" Murine soothes. "You are as close now to the Hound as you will ever come. I promised you a feast, did I not?"

"The likes of which we've never tasted."

"The likes of which this *city* has never tasted! And now, if all are ready, we shall proceed to the savoury. A walnut liqueur and the very crown of the meal, a genuine Combalou Roquefort!"

"And what's that on the side?"

"Cold tongue."

Pink turns somewhat paler. Whiskers jabs him in the ribs. "Don't you dare leave a crumb!"

Words of wisdom, for even in a city operating under the *lex talionis*, *habeas corpus* remains the rule.

Part III
Biohazard

Into the Mist

The Traveller

It's time that you were moving on, the afternoon is past,
the leaves are whispering in the breeze and shadows lie askance.
A game can always be rejoined; all games are one, at last,
and thus to leave them guessing now will even up the chance.
Oh, ask not how the journey starts, nor ask where it shall end,
but know you are the Traveller, and that the road shall bend.

Upon the side that's sinister, night rises from the sea,
its banners raised, outflying, bear the pristine evening star.
Upon the right hand sunlight's lances seek the enemy,
strike at the shadows and the mist and all reflections bar;
and in the sky between the war has set the clouds aflame,
smouldering into colours that no human tongue can name.

And throughout the wrack you pass,
change's agent, first and last,
as the allies of the daylight
range along the western walls
of the house that stands alone,
as the sun's remaining throne;
they hail approaching midnight
with defiant trumpet calls.
Such suspicion brings this light,
as within a dream, a flight.
All you can recall are traces,
the imperatives are gone.
But you're standing at the gate
and the time is growing late,
secret paths and dang'rous places
mark the way you travel on.

The wind from the horizon brings the rumours of a fall,
you know there will be hunters now sent out from either side;
you know that there are monsters, in your time you've faced them all,
and he that is beloved does not travel at your side,
but you know greater things will come than all that yet has been.
The star is riding high now but your path is still unseen.

Around you, they are racing; people fleeing from the change.
Keep walking, keep you walking on, you'll never pay the toll.
The leaves unfurl their hearts for dusk on flowers pale and strange,
their perfume steals upon the air as dreams upon the soul;
the scent of one beloved from a sunlit garden blown,
and if you could but glimpse him you might lay your burden down.

But when you attain the hill,
he retreats before you still.
Broken hands and crumbling faces,
such mementos feel no pain.
So it is you sit once more
in the shadow of a door
that the ivy now embraces,
and lay out the cards again.
It would feel so good to weep
and to bow your head, and sleep;
but 'tis in such coin the night pays
out the waking dream of gold.
And you know to never eat
in the place you take your seat,
and a room that has two doorways
is a room that cannot hold.

A shadow glimpsed, a footstep heard that leaves no other trace;
the hunters come a-hunting but pursue your trail in vain.
The clouds run out like ribbons or like cuts across a face,
the colours smoulder low and ash to other names again.

And now the endless battle's won, and now the light is dying,
Traveller, lay your burden down and leave your burden lying.

The house has set the rules for this, the game is very sure.
There's air to kiss your fingers, cooled in cavern-darkness sweet.
The memory of a feather moon within the deep azure
make dreams lose their distinction as the trees in shadows meet.
And still the journey keeps you from becoming lost as well,
you go and you keep going, going further than you tell.

The Grandchild

Its brick
coated thick
with dust, stands a sepulchre,
that hosts a kind of life.
Dry eye
is glazed by
the sun; sleeping stillness like
a heart touched by the knife.
So kind,
never mind.
Hands embalmed but it does not
stop the decay, the creeping rot
behind the amber, blind-dog gumming
discs; and yet a smile is coming,
withered back with the repeat
of Ma's complaint that she won't eat.
A small thing,
crouching,
and wondering if curses can be real.

Slow sun
falling on
the gloss-smiling magazines.
A gentle laugh, so wise.
Soft talk,
they don't baulk;
it's in the name of hygiene
and the packaging is nice.
Sits each
in their niche.
Like cuts the laughter frees her mouth

and through the chatter, words slide out
like blood into the sacral bowl
that stains the blade as black as coal.
Such clear corruption breaks the pact:
the victim smiles, they halt the act.
A dark thing,
hunching,
and wondering if curses can be real.

Backed up,
the clocks tuck
minutes back into the fold.
Shadow tints the arc
of cloud fret-
ted air, yet
comes the blanket, amber glow,
blanking out the dark.
Clocks beat
day's retreat
and in the television's cage
they slump and smile and show their age,
and then Papa takes up Ma's hand
and leads her out onto the land-
ing, pointing out at the unknown.
Where the street lamps gleam, alone,
the cursed thing,
dancing,
exulting in her own, dark weal.

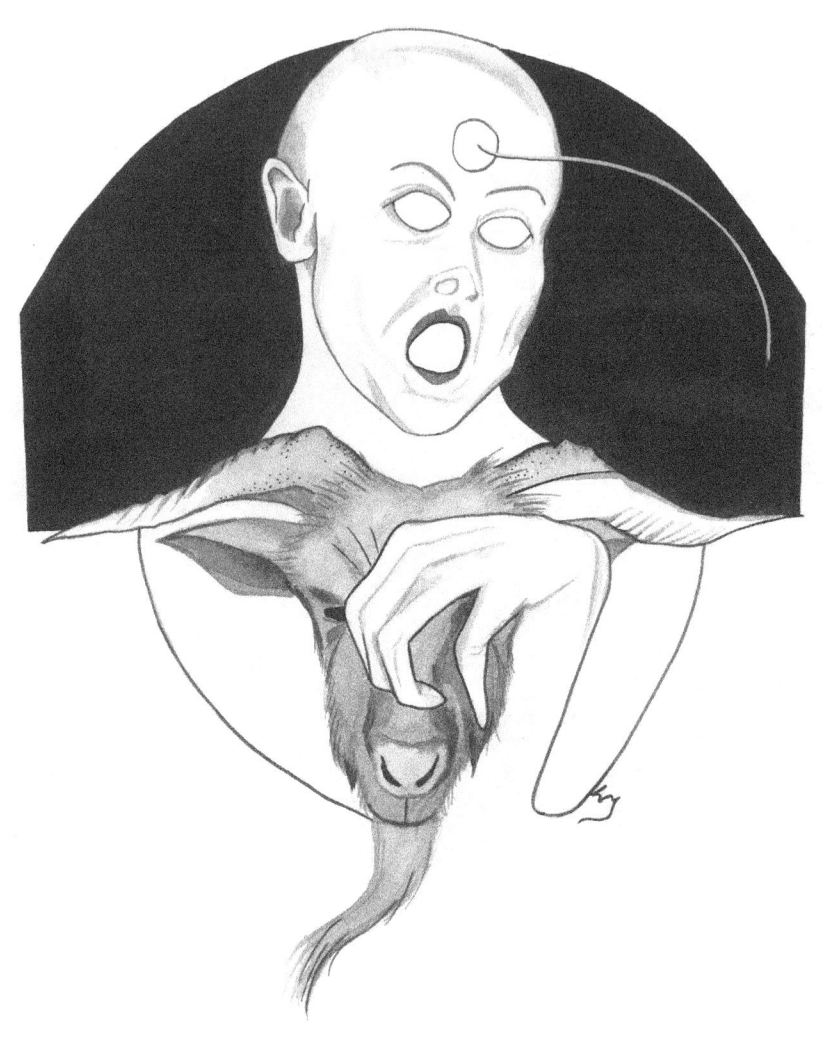

Scapegoat

The Sleep of Reason (interrupted)

There is a bell
ringing on the midnight wind, if you're listening.
The sleep in your eyes
gives life to shadows on the floor. Window glistening.
What do you hear?
Rain falls like tears, like a hand on your heart,
a pledge you've never known
is dashed against the pane.
But you're alone.
How could you let these fancies start again?
For the simplest things will speak,
when the night is running deep.
The veil is thinnest in the darkest season,
when a basin and a jug,
sheaf of arrows and a glove,
weigh heavy on the chest of Reason.

Faint is your heart
and helpless are your hands, welded to the chair.
The pulse of your blood
is rising in a fever's dance, whispering *who's there?*
You've lost control.
On the last chime, they burst open the door;
cry out for lost and found!
They dance and draw you on!
Silence surrounds.
How can you curse and bid them to be gone?
For the strangest things will speak,
when the night is running deep,
and all the senses conspire in treason.

In the circle, fire burns
as the agony returns
to paralyse the limbs of Reason.

Exorcism

I conjure thee, oh spectre of belief,
thou fractured multiple, father of conflict and mother of lies.
Leave these feeble bodies and minds weakened by love,
by hatred and fear of the unknown.
In the name of science self-examining, the sole perfectible,
appear before us now (in no alarming form); obey
the rod of measurement and that observant ring
through which the unseen is manifest. Appear!
That they may witness the power of the one
that casts the false priest from the temple
and strikes the black magician down.

I adjure thee, by the repetition of results
and mathematical models, by which we borrow years,
return now to the outer darkness
which we recognise as the darkness of our inner mind;
unconscious impulse, the residue of evolution.
The definition compels thee to the norm!
By the sacred names, that thou cannot fail to obey:
Serotonin! Hippocampus! Hypothalamus!
The meaning is the mechanism: that is all.
Let the rational rejoice.

I exorcise thee, that answers may be singular,
laws immutable and the dead stay dead.
Only flood and earthquake disturb our nights;
their causes sure, our response prescribed. We rest,
secure in the knowledge that there is no other:
only the average of processes we all share
and certain gendered traits. And on that great day
when time itself shall cease, we shall join each other,
the animals, our earth and the stars themselves

in thermodynamic cessation.
We have calculated this and as it must be,
desire it, for it is the measure of peace. Let all
take comfort in the ultimate end of truth.

The Sculptor

The door's too thin, the noise gets in;
the light's white noise and heat.
The sculptor knits half-forms and sits
and shudders, every beat.
To see and plan and work with an
uncomprehending heart.
To see her matter mastered at a
curious plastic art!
"Did I not master sandstone?
Do I not control the clay?
Nor set the shapes for wood and bone?
In this room I dare say
out loud, I am proud
as the slate of Rome.
So why is it I
cannot rest alone?
Impassive, you, as
the marble of Greece,
cleverly never
leaving me in peace!"

The walls are high and warded by
the figures of her schemes,
ten steps apace, a breathing space:
they don't keep out the dreams.
A word exchanged, a meet arranged
to show appreciation,
how could that give her visions with
unruly animation?
"Is not the marble flesh enough?

Bonescape

Is not the bronze the life?
Why can't I work this massy stuff
with either pick or knife?
Eyes close on stone rose,
lacing round the light,
in place is your face
blazing day and night!
Creeps ka back to sar-
cophagus in sand.
This too, I would do
just to kiss your hand!"

"I no more hold to build idols,
I broke the ones I'd made.
I have annealed all my ideals,
in steel they stand displayed.
It is a deal to work in steel!
The best, in all my pride,
I ever did, this caryatid
that holds the ceiling high!"
And so she works within her shrine,
so sure her touch on stone,
yet does not dare that precious line,
from cheek to collarbone.
Scholar, courtier,
sculpturesque in jade,
would be mockery,
before all displayed!
Tracing and pacing,
turn about the floor –
there's knocking at the door.
There's knocking at the door!

Virgins and Martyrs

The vision of white and red roses blooming among thorns at once calls up a symbolic assimilation in the medieval mind: for example, that of virgins and martyrs, shining with glory in the midst of their persecutors.
—J. Huizinga, *The Waning of the Middle Ages*

> They hang from the thorn there,
> the Virgins and Martyrs;
> so many have borne their
> unholy stigmata.
> Curtsey to the altar the girls all in white,
> for men in black robes appreciate the sight.
> They want it so pure, so sweet and so sad,
> and isn't it sick that they want it so bad,
> that they destroy souls to get what they need.
> They've only one chance for we're white till we bleed.
> We're white till we bleed.
> So fragile, so tender,
> could bruise with a finger.
> Not much, is there,
> between touch and tear?
> If I'm to be with you,
> must I bring roses?
> Staining the linen who-
> ever proposes?
>
> They hang by the door there,
> the Virgins and Martyrs,
> Madonna and whore share
> *in nomine patris.*
> Should I fold my hands now and bow down my head,
> and receive the Lord at the foot of the bed?
> Opened, a woman's a horror unclean,

so spit where you shot and then boast where you've been.
You can't cleanse the stain, you can't stem the flood,
for this is my body and this is my blood.
Yes, this is my blood.
To make our communion,
I'll bring it to you in
this cup, with a knife.
Drink the waters of life.
But you'll share with me, love,
as I share your need,
you'll bleed with me, my love,
I'll make you bleed.

Adoration

Vespers

For David

Blest be he who shuts my eyes
and who would place his hands on me.
Who in this dread hour would dare?
To touch the skin and part the hair,
the hands compose in stillness; he
stirs me enough to be aware
that he is here and cares for me.

Blest be he who veils my face,
who comes between me and the light.
For him is all my body laid,
the tender bound in bone and braid,
in loop and lace; a seemly sight
and every pain he sees displayed,
let him embrace without respite.

Blest be he who lays him down
to wait the night out at my side.
Enfolding me he is in turn
entwined, for he cannot unlearn
what he has known. All else belied,
still in this hour, for eterne
he—I alone will here abide.

Day Cars

It's Saturday and the traffic is horrendous,
the volume is tremendous and I'm sick with fear.
The first question is, where is everybody going?
The second, envisage, how did I end up here?
Is this the way? God's sake, why aren't I moving?
What do I think I'm proving with these jumps and jars?
When you touch twenty-six and the engine's stalling,
in the midst of the traffic you'll see these cars
glide through the streets and the roads and the highways,
gleaming with chrome and discreet smoked glass.
They move in procession, without haste and without delays.
They move in procession and so solemnly pass.

It must be an occasion to sit inside one,
dark windows to hide unknown celebrity
and though the circumstance may disconcert you,
it's fair to make a virtue of necessity.
It's natural that there be some trepidation
marking every station that our bodies go,
but the glove and the veil your anxiety shall assuage
and so smooth is the passage you won't even know.
They know the routes, the two routes given,
the long, sleek cars in their silver sheathes
and the only difference is the colour of the ribbon,
the only difference is the flowers in the wreathes.

White roses, however, make for some confusion,
an unthinkable collusion of identity,
but it can't be red if the party is a funeral
and neither for a wedding as the case may be.
Grandparents die, and people our age get married
though the motion may be carried in the inverse way;

in which case tragedy, and the old fool's hoping
but the cars will be recouping on the slight delay.
We are aware and this is monstrous,
clocking the kilometres we have alive.
We are not natural until you bury us,
we are not natural and I can't drive.

My Guest

The light is running from the sky
like syrup from a broken glass.
I see there is a sallow cast
to every face; there was a dye
and now a nothing takes its place.
At this sign, I will go inside,
I will unbind and comb my hair.
I take the books from off the chair
next to my bed, that stands beside
me like a nurse with bowèd head.
Could she have brought this glass to me?
I'll have no medicine in this room
and no light in the deepening gloom.
Between the curtain rings I see
plain nothing, and yet I am certain
that my guest can redeem it all.
My invitation is unspoken,
as I slide the window open,
tie curtains right against the wall,
and turn the chair round for the night.
Welcome darkness, welcome daemon
that holds my soul within its hands.
Come sit by me, we will make plans
to rise and overthrow. You came on
silent wings; soon, all the world shall know.

Hymn

Do you know what they did to him?
In the early dawn, they drove him from the temple,
not speaking his crime, only truisms of revenge.
Took away his spear and royal garb,
gave him the head of an ass and severed it,
let the beast bleed out upon the sand.
Flayed the skin and took it to the marketplace.
Sold it to the foreigners, tainted already by blood;
to the foulness of foreigners, exiled him forever.

They modelled his body in wax, a parody
shaped by crude fingers: he, the most beautiful!
His proud face and curling hair, eyes like spearheads,
reduced to this! Probed by a priest like a rude boy,
removing parts like a rude boy.
As the sun rose they exposed him
like a deformed child, to the desert.
Like a condemned man, to the desert.
Melted into the sand, into the formless mass forever.

And they were right to do this, else
one would have slain his master, another his mate.
The third proclaimed the scrolls of doctrine folly.
The fourth abandoned his station to go amongst the slaves
and war would have come of that: the fifth
would have cast his lust in marble, sculpting a vision
to damn men for a thousand years. The sixth dissected corpses.
As it was their sins were little, measured in
a broken jar, woman's tears, and piss in a well.

It was left for her to love him.
To collect the potsherds and draw the forbidden shape,

to make the offering and take refuge in the darkness.
As the black leaves whisper and the veil lifts,
to remember wings and fire, a night sky and a circle dance,
a beating heart and be free. If this should mean another's bed,
a husband cold in hers, or stilling the second heart
beating in her belly, so it must be.
He accepts no supplicant on their knees.

And if the leaves and shadows cannot hide her,
she will die as he did and be glad.
Small price for the knowledge that sets strength free from body,
beauty from approval, desire from expectation.
Power free from the order of men.
The soul free from the order of gods.
To home in the desert, beyond the border
each enemy lays upon the other. To suffer and heal,
to die and be born, to cross and return.

That is the dance and each day, each night,
each year, each age, we dance it. On black wings
the change comes, however small. However poor
compared to the sin denied. However slow,
men learn of freedom. Learn to despise
only he that claimed both sisters, bringing light and shadow
under his dominion, and judgement to the eternal between.
For no slave can love him. None who does not look
beyond the father's thou shalt not, the mother's cannot be.

Descend then the black steps that were first of all.
Open your arms to the serpent, your breast to the thorns.
In the circle of leaves and the circle of stone
the fire burns, and the heart seized in his hand is yours.
There in the garden, in the serpents and thorns,
in the sand and the darkness, the scars and the head,
in strength and in beauty, in love and in pride,
in triumph beyond all borders—the veil descends,
and I am left with symbols and a name.

The Sleep of Reason (concluded)

The white tower rose
and the brethren's castle fell, over aeons' span.
I died at their hands
and at my own: in youth, in age, as woman and man.
Such things to say!
I saw his eyes, took the cup from his hands,
a thousand lives too few
to wash such love away!
Could it be true?
If this is real, how can I bear the day?
For the strongest things will speak
when the night is running deep,
and ancient memories rise to test their prison.
So tell yourself you dream:
ever darkly speeds the stream
and heavy is the sleep of Reason.
Deathly is the sleep of Reason.

Part IV

The Feast of Mistrust

The Festival

I. The Fear

Hark the bells in the bright air!
Calling the people nigh
as mass begins, to lay their sins
before the Virgin's shrine.
The year she lies encoffined, seven shrouds of darkened wood
but seven locks are open now to do the city good.

An ancient place, this city,
beyond its present name.
A single street where rivers meet
was once its only fame.
Reeds grew upon the flatland and a green hill rose above,
but too much blood has wasted here for anything but love.

The myth concerns two brothers
and the goddess of the flow,
who bright renown and lineage down
the ages would bestow.
One gifted her with horses, artefacts of bronze and tin.
The winner fed the waters with the bodies of his kin.

His descendents kept the pact
with columns, marble white.
The open space a marketplace,
a temple on the height.
And then they bridged the rivers: and the moment this was done,
a foreign army marched across and slaughtered every one.

These others were pragmatic:
they built a double wall,
inlaid black slate before the gate
and in their chieftain's hall;

Who put away his former wife, disowned her son who then
returned home with new allies won and slaughter, once again.

Time after time it happened!
They purged with blade and flame,
they raised higher dome and spire,
then ended up the same.
Perhaps that's why the Virgin does so many hopes revive,
for in the wreck of history, 'tis women who survive.

Pride is a city's proper sin,
its history recited,
why so and so were laid below
while such and such were knighted.
Each race has left its layer of legendry and conjecture,
reducing all their struggles to intriguing architecture.

Pride is a city's proper sin
for dignity and wealth
require the signs of ships and mines –
witness the church itself!
The altar piece is golden and the altar marble-stepped,
but underneath the grand façade, there is a secret kept.

From eyes and ears and open maws
that cling to turret stone,
to carven head and sealing lead
that holds the dust and bone.
Ah, slow the church is sinking; it is but the dead who know
there's inches less in crypt and rat-hole than a year ago.

The dead do not look upward
but turn their eyes below,
to watch a deliquescence well
from out the dark; as though
this single fear remains to them, when everything they knew
has been as they are, buried, overladen by the new.

Under us in layers lies
the flesh that history lacks.
Take care to stand, tread lightly and,
dear God, avoid the cracks!
Stratum at first translucent clouding with the final breath,
of all the myriads caught at the moment of their death.

****

Lady Webbe can see the dead,
her blessing and her curse.
A doom to know what lies below;
to not know would be worse.
She takes all due precautions and with care her route will choose,
making good use of bridges and unlikely platform shoes.

Greying hair beneath the veil,
her gown of dusty hue;
brocaded vest sharing the crest
upon her family pew.
She nods to those who near her in a manner calm and wise,
the hanging lace a shield before her lens-faceted eyes.

No more now the frightened child
who would not touch the floor,
earning the curse of maid and nurse
for what she said she saw.
No more the girl who spent her days atop the highest tower,
failing to gain a husband, even with substantial dower.

In her case particular
the must of fear and laughter,
as grapes to wine, produced in time
a researcher and author,
generally disregarded, although those who make critique
agree unhesitating her perspective is unique.

But Doctor Wulf would differ,
in marching up the aisle

with hat and cane, silvery mane
and supercilious smile.
He thinks the style of Lady Webbe is not a scholar's fancy,
but evinces the usage of the blackest necromancy.

A hunter is Doctor Wulf
of oft-contested game.
Neither a priest nor scientist
would now support his claim.
But he has seen the devil leering from a young girl's eyes,
and heard the Beast exultant as the moon began to rise.

He has battled monsters, with
sedative, strap and knife;
turned hypnotist and theurgist
to save innocent life;
and travelled far in many lands pursuing sacred truth,
of why such things may be and, failing that, a little proof.

Lately, memories of home
haunting his hoary head,
he did his mind only to find
exactly what he fled –
a city fraught with rumour of the weakling or unwise
who vanish altogether; else are found without their eyes.

Lady Webbe has fashioned
a volume bound, he thinks,
in human skin, to write within,
with blood and tears her inks.
In confidence of holy ground, he'll beard her in her den,
test her resolve with riddles raised and see what follows then.

"Greetings to you, Lady Webbe,
upon this hallowed morn!
I trust I may such greeting say,
although I have forgone

a formal introduction: I'm familiar with your work,
acknowledging a challenge that a lesser man would shirk."

"But I do know you, Doctor,
a healer of repute.
You tend the mad and that you've had
results few would dispute!
Apart from this I dare say that we met once long ago,
within a room where wedding guests were never meant to go."

Doctor Wulf, he frowns and says,
"I fear you have mistook.
I'm not a one for feast and fun,
I much prefer a book!
Which brings us back to something I would ask despite my fears
of being thought impudent: where do you get your ideas?"

"Answering that is simple; why,
I find them on the floor!
Where such as I have laid them by
from many years before.
But here comes the procession, as occasion does befit,
and if you have not finished, then I think you'd better sit."

The bishop now approaches
in such sanctity arrayed
as will impress all those who dress
in feather, lace and braid.
Gold is his cope and mitre, and an alb of spotless white
is trimmed with pearl and emerald, and ruby winking bright.

His pallid face is flattened
by solemness—at best
a twitching eye and mouth marked by
a slit, four holes the rest.
Before him boys bear candles and behind they hold his train,
with silver voices raising to the vault, the old refrain.

"Oh pearl of the pure waters!
　Star of the clearest sky!
　Oh maiden free of macle we
　beseech thee, hear our cry!
　Oh wipe the sins from out our souls and tears from out our eyes,
　and let us drink thy precious draught, one day in paradise."

"Why do you smile, Lady Webbe,
　as though they do amuse?"
"It's amazing that what they sing
　so many things confuse!
　This church was once a temple to the goddess of the stream,
　which makes the dedication more complex than it might seem."

"Lady Webbe, you cannot mean
　to draw comparison
　between our grand religion and
　a gross superstition!"
"All that I do is state a fact which anyone can see
　who takes the time to finely view the lower masonry.

"Those columns there are recent
　but rise on ancient piles –
　the very span the brothers ran!
　These deep-worn marble tiles
　still bear her name and symbol; and the question yet remains,
　of what exactly's in that box they bind with locks and chains."

"Lady, I fear you trifle
　with matters grim and grave.
　Those who their fault would set at naught
　are difficult to save!"
"Your words perplex me, Doctor, but there're others I would hear.
　Would you disturb the bishop? Now be quiet, there's a dear."

　Bejewelled hands extended
　quiet the murmuring.

The crowd no longer talk among
  themselves, no children sing.
"Before me now I contemplate the town's entirety,
  the high seats, homes and hovels all proceeding to the quay!

"Standing here I look upon
  the heroes of our state,
  women refined in heart and mind,
  the offspring of the great,
  adorned with understanding and arrayed in dignity.
  I look upon all this and say alas, what wretches we!

"Can any person here claim
  to have avoided sin?
  We must forgive all those who live
  above a day within
  this world of ours, so rich in all that stirs the appetite,
  so ripe with opportunity for sensual delight.

"The day draws near when we shall
  envy the deaf and blind!
  Lust only for the plain and poor,
  set sloth and wrath behind!
  From out of our long-buried past, its horrors and duress,
  we may anticipate the punishment for our excess!

"So this night we hold a feast
  but not to slake our thirst,
  neither to feed the glutted greed
  of belly or of purse.
  It is to show contrition, so that God may set aside
  the doom of the one rising flame and all-consuming tide!"

A tremor troubles the veil
shielding the lady's face,
although her hand gripping the stand
firmly remains in place.

It might well seem the bishop's words have struck a fearful chord,
although this intimation is by Doctor Wulf ignored.

Doctor Wulf is troubled
by visions of his own.
A boy who fled the newly wed
and thought to be alone,
perturbed was to discover, deep inside the library,
a girl in glasses that perused an antique bestiary.

Good Doctor Wulf remembers
speaking harshly to this girl
and her reply in accents dry
caused all his hairs to curl.
They started a discussion of the comparative risk
of fronting the Medusa as opposed the basilisk.

Meanwhile the bishop rambles,
the congregation learn
that their Virgin forgives the sin
of all who do not burn.
"It is she who brings us comfort in our hour of release,
so with that thought before you now, go forth in joy and peace."

And as the congregation stand,
the doctor fails to see
the lady quail to lift her veil
and turn her gaze beneath.
And when she does it is as though all time comes to a stop,
to see the burning man is that much closer to the top.

Some fears belong to childhood,
phantasms we forget
but nothing can be stronger than
those that pursue us yet.
His eyes devoured by the flame that wreathes about his brow
like laurels crown a hero, though cruel chains surround him now.

A star he first seemed to her,
trapped deep within the hill,
where stratum fold that which is old
upon the older still.
While others are suspended in the amber of their hour,
with what an agony he moves, with what terrible power.

Is it her fault he rises?
For exactly such fears
she sought to tame, seeking his name
through many books and years,
as though her search has summoned him through centuries to press
against the last meniscus in his ultimate duress.

And so to the bishop she
will take her fear at last.
There will not be apology
for their contentions past.
The matter of his sermon has recalled a hope long-flown,
that as a witness to the dead, she does not stand alone.

Doctor Wulf startles to see
the height his mark obtains.
He too would stand except his hand
a sudden plaintiff claims.
A child draped in a cassock on which wax has clotted cold,
with sorrow that such tender eyes are not designed to hold.

"Why, child, what can trouble you
 with all the feast before?
 Come speak to me, you plainly see
 that I am a doctor."
"Indeed, Sir: it is you I seek! My Ma is very ill
 and we have found no remedy in potion, 'press or pill!

"She's a cook, Sir, and today
 is her profession's crown.

But scream she does, and claw at us!
We had to tie her down!
She tore my sister's face and struck our father in the chest,
but would not touch my vestments or the ring the bishop blest.

"If you would deign, good doctor,
to visit us below,
We will obey whatever may
be what you say is so!
The pies and cake shall not be baked, we shall not see a crumb!
We live beside the river; in the Virgin's name, do come!"

Time was when he would indeed
wander the waterside,
treating the poor for nothing more
than a practitioner's pride.
"Oh, say no more my charming boy, but lead me with all haste.
If what I do suspect is true, there is no time to waste!"

Strangely pangs the lady's heart
to see him led away
by figure that, in cape and hat,
apes his as children may.
But yet resolved, she seeks the chamber where the bishop dresses,
stepping across the sunken ghosts of his nine predecessors.

Round the ambulatory
she teeters, under lace
of stone and glass, a master class
in every grotesque face.
A heretic intruding where the pious would not dream,
and thus she is the closest when the bishop starts to scream.

Another vision, she assumes,
accustomed to the sight
of corpse's flesh, that it is fresh
can simply not be right!

But anyone could see the naked body lying there,
a boy with sockets for his eyes and wax caught in his hair.

And as smoke from cooking stoves
creates a gloomy pall,
from out the door penitents pour,
down the processional.
A city with a debt of blood, a city built for show,
with groaning stone upon its crown and only reeds below.

And as the lady reaches out,
and as the doctor fails
to spot pretence, the cooks commence
with rolling pins and scales,
with broken glass and fishhooks, with fruit putrid and diseased,
with ergot and datura, they are preparing the feast.

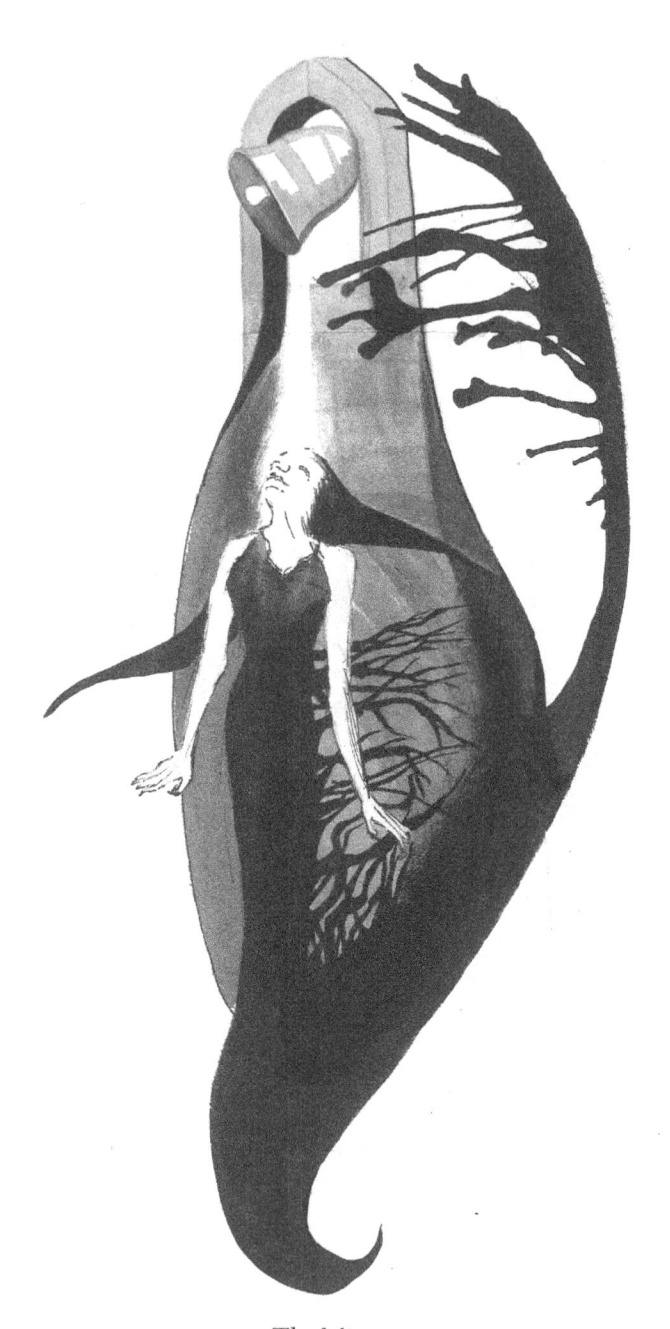

The Mistress

ii. The Fare

From those first monoliths raised
upon the bleak hillside,
a city grew where each man knew
fortune pursues the tide.
From those who gather oysters to the owners of the ship
that brings the wine and spices: all are in the river's grip.

And there lies a paradox
few people seem to note.
All those who count had rather mount
a dais than a boat.
The higher in the hierarchy, the higher up the hill,
and further from the water with its miasmatic chill.

Here, the houses huddle close
on cliffs and islands wrought
as stone decays to leave a maze
of mud and gravel, fraught
still further by the beggars, and each cozener and cove
who extricates a living out of what falls from above.

Doctor Wulf has dared far worse
to follow his crusade,
but his young escort would seem less
at home and more afraid
as they approach a humble house cut in the very rock,
with bars across the windows and upon the door a lock.

Nonetheless escapes a scent
of nutmeg and of cloves,
of vanilla and ginger jar
and something more than those;

whiff of familiarity, a place once smelt before.
Good Doctor Wulf, he doffs his hat and passes through the door.

Saucepans gleam upon the wall,
the wood waits in the hearth
and in the midst a woman sits
bound in a copper bath,
acknowledging his presence with a spray of bloody foam,
while eyes as mad as broken eggs revolve about her home.

A bandaged face attends her,
teasing at tangled hair.
A doleful man attempts to fan
the candy-scented air.
"Oh Papa, I have brought him! Quickly, let our mother see!"
Whereon a voice like creeping fire kindles: "It is he!"

Can she see him? Still her eyes
are rolling round and round.
Stepping closer: if he knows her
the change is more profound
than Lady Webbe; or is it not the woman but the *thing*
that has displaced the proper soul that so addresses him?

"Say then what you want of me
but warned be—I will not
assent to your possession or
this woman's sorry lot!"
"Those are the very words," it flares, "you spake the day you took
my servant and reduced her from an oracle to cook!"

"How long have I waited for
you, doctor, to return?
The hero who such things can do,
the mistress shall not spurn!"
"But I know *you*!" the doctor cries. "'Twas just such nonsense wild
Lucia raved so long ago!" And then he sees the child.

From either side fingers dig
into the skull: so calm
the chorist' stands, raising both hands,
an eye upon each palm!
No boy here but an agèd man with hunched and crookèd back,
and in his wrinkled face a pair of sockets gaping black.

Gasping, Doctor Wulf falls back
against the bath, to feel
those feet and hands, like living bands,
draw him into a reel!
Still bound herself the madwoman sears joy into his ear:
"Soon now the master shall be free, at last the day is here!"

****

Far above the doctor's plight,
the steeple points at noon.
Canon and deacon peer to see,
then gasp and sob, or swoon.
What leaven can there be for this, what balm allay the truth,
that mother church is no preserve of innocence and youth?

Lady Webbe will not remit
the bishop to despair.
Holding his cope much like a rope
she leads him up the stair
to where the very bells reside and earth is far below.
She turns upon the trembling man and cries, "What do you know?"

"I know much," the bishop says,
"of man's depravity.
Such knowledge learned cannot be burned
or drowned beneath the sea!
It must emerge at last," he says, at which the lady sighs.
"Your Grace, the sermon's over: now, about those missing eyes!

"Are you aware that simil-
ar crimes have taken place
across our history? This is
known as the *master's face*.
A gruesome sect devoted to the darkest sorcery;
although they all were thought to have been hung last century."

"You know them?" the bishop gasps,
recovers then his poise.
"Such disrespect I would correct,
would you but heed my voice!
To treat this like a tale from out your scandalous histories:
the boy is yet unburied! Now, unhand my vestments please!"

"No, not yet," says Lady Webbe,
"that isn't good enough.
It would be more accurate for
me to say I know *of*
these miscreants, pursuing them through reference and clue.
But I can't boast a personal acquaintance yet. Can *you?*"

The bishop gapes. "I'm certain,
I read as much as you!
But have the wisdom to, in this,
distinguish false from true!"
"That may be by the standards of this self-deluding town,
but we are far beyond that now. Look down, your Grace, look down!"

Down concentric rings of streets,
cut through with bridge and stair;
over cresset and minaret
and through the tainted air;
they gaze upon lost symbol, missing key and secret mark,
and at the tables being set in every place and park.

Tying off the bell-rope and
throwing a loop about

the bishop's waist, she's fairly placed
to hoist him up and out!
His face no more a china plate that serves up homilies,
confronted by a death that might be his, the bishop *sees*.

His life flashes past his eyes:
a most cruel revelation!
For vertigo, all adepts know
enhances concentration.
He sees again the path he took to reach his present height:
it's strewn with lies and treachery, and jagged-edged despite.

No vision of the buried
torments his bulging eyes,
and yet he screams because it seems
that the true horror lies
within the childhood that he fled so many years before,
and if there is a balm, it's that the lady sees still more.

"No!" she cries, "this cannot be!
We spoke an hour past!
If he is dead, then what we said
will never be surpassed!
But were he dead, he would not lie so low within the hill.
He's at the threshold of the Deep, and yet I see him still!"

"*Oracle!*" the bishop shrieks,
with memories ablaze.
"I see it true! It's you, it's you!
Haunting me all my days!
I swore I'd never wear your mask nor serve the master blind,
but if I can't out climb you then to fall I am resigned!"

Snaring a handful of veil
he loops it round and round,
swearing an oath to bring them both
crashing upon the ground!

"An oracle you're calling me? A priestess of some sort?
I'm sure I'm nothing of the kind! Your Grace, just hold that thought!"

****

Why are the bells ringing now,
mass is away and done?
Many below would like to know:
the doctor is not one.
The doctor is preoccupied with whether he will drown,
tied as he is, by hand and foot, and bobbing up and down.

As yet he breathes a fetor,
bubbling against his skin,
as in the dark many a spark
begins to swirl and spin
in patterns that the mad might read with perfect clarity,
and colours corpses might compound, to show their sympathy.

He lives: he is sure he lives,
unless death be a door
with iron band surrounded and
set in a cellar floor.
Which way the head? Which way the foot of this uncanny well?
With but his own for reference, he has no way to tell.

Is he mad? Possibly but
the thought itself is clear,
unlike the sound from all around
that seeps into his ear.
"Awake now, whist now: what is this? A shape, a shape it be!
With edges here and edges there, so wrap it round and see."

Darkness flows, condenses and
quickly solidifies,
like fingers pressed against his chest
and seeking lips and eyes.

A thousand fingers! Voices trickle, suppurate and ooze:
"Oh edges, edges out of place: what is it, then, or whose?"

Answering would seem unwise
expenditure of air,
but Doctor Wulf confronts the gulf
without apparent care.
"Be you another or the same: be all the same or no,
by Heaven's grace thou demon, I demand you let me go!"

Voices shiver, drip and drool:
"Nothing, no one, I vow,
escapes from me, no trickery
will keep you from me now!
For you I know; yes, now I do, your form at last is free!
I hold you, kiss you: come my love, come back and lie with me."

Cold caress becomes a pull
and not towards the top!
Orientated by this strait
he thrashes, tries to stop
his foul, inexorable descent with naught but will and fear,
as all the while the voices plead: "Come back, come back, my dear!"

A knocking, unlocking sound:
a circle shimmers bright.
A figure dim is hauling him
upwards towards the light!
Resisting, writhing, hollering, he fights the undertow
seeking to reunite him with all corruption below.

Upon his first breath of air,
ceases the Deep to draw,
so he over his rescuer
tumbles across the floor.
"Quietly," begs a voice, at odds with the main strength displayed.
"I have a dish to fit you, and a pie-crust freshly made."

Grateful as he is for this
expedient release,
such a proposal does not go
to set a man at ease.
Still fettered, he contrives to raise his head from out the straw
and finally discerns a face of which he can be sure.

"Lucia! Can it be that
the girl who I set free
from demon's claw so long before
has come to rescue me?
They had you wrapped in bandages: I see the marks, but why
do you now succour me if you were party to the lie?"

Grave in her apron and cap,
and granite in her build,
she gives him lift, although this gift
is not so kindly willed.
"Why, Sir, I say you made me sane, and so I cannot bear
to see a living man given to what lies under there.

"In truth, Sir, I should avenge
myself upon your head!
My family dismisses me
as one already dead.
But even so, I must redeem the author of my pain
and risk their greater anger through the curse of being sane."

Bobbing now beneath her arm,
the doctor would protest.
Surely her state does not equate
to those so sore oppressed?
"The outer symptoms of my case were all that met your eye;
you cannot judge unless you have once been as mad as I.

"I have seen the centuries pass
like waves beneath a prow,

felt the embrace of he whose face
my father mimics now.
To knead and bake, to stuff and slake can scarcely assuage me!
Although the feast provides a kind of outlet, as you see."

As about the doctor sounds
of water surge and ebb,
it seems that he seriously
misjudged the Lady Webbe.
Everything that experience disposes him to fear
from the practitioners of death is in this kitchen here.

Abominations in jars
and desiccate remains:
such herbs as will not only kill
but madden human brains.
Stingers and pods and tentacles; small spiders, quite alive,
are set beside the toffee for Lucia to arrive.

When he sees the destined dish,
he struggles to break free.
The psychopath has left her bath
for his incumbency.
"Be quiet now, you silly man! Do you want them to know?
Did I not tell you I was sane? Oh stop it: in you go!"

****

Does the lady glimpse the ghost
of his apology?
Perhaps she does, although she is
concerned tangentially,
explaining how a violent gust of wind the crisis brought
and haply in the bell-rope both His Grace and she were caught.

The bishop fails to contest
this version of events;
in fact he do seem eager to

assist in the pretence,
assuring priest and laity that all in fact is well
and that to try and bar his way will merit time in Hell.

"Hell lies on the waterfront?"
She whispers past her hand.
"That you repress such an address
I well can understand,
but lead me there this day, I beg! And furthermore explain,
if all their women see like me, why I am not insane."

Free now of the faithful who
are giving thanks above,
he mutters, "Yes, but you I bless
for that portentous shove!
And likewise for the fiction that it was the wind, not I,
that set us swinging in the ropes. As for your madness, why!

"You have not known the master;
simple enough to see,
although the knot you'd tied was what
it took to convince me!"
The bishop leads her up the aisle and out the chapter door,
displaying in the golden light the city all before.

Something shifts beneath their feet
that should not shift at all.
The solid ground should not rebound,
shaking the walks and walls.
An instant only: but enough to see the lady take
a gasping breath and for the bishop's new resolve to shake.

In the plaza women bend
and workmen set their hand
to chasing what has spilled from pot
and righting fallen stand.

The preparations for the feast will not be set aside
for any danger that can be so readily denied.

"Has it begun?" The bishop clasps
his hands in fervent prayer.
"O Virgin sweet, let those who eat
appease your wrath and spare
the mostly mild majority, who mainly would not do
the kind of malfeasance that is offensive unto you!"

"I would guess," the lady says,
"our sins are not the cause.
Things are amiss in that abyss
which underlies our floors.
For though we save the doctor from your vicious family,
I must confront the nemesis which has so haunted me!"

So bright the eyes beneath her,
so fierce the flame that burns,
such as will make the good earth shake
when he at last returns.
She cannot shift a single inch; her heels are leaden weights,
as though the flesh solidifies where earth evaporates.

"Go!" she cries. "You must be quick!
I can no longer see
Wulf there below: I do not know
if he is lost or free.
But this recall: myths often place the truth behind a veil.
I fear a grimmer meaning to our ancient fairy tale!"

Every year upon this night
since history began,
a festival surviving all
that changes time and man
has taken place and any who might know the reason why,
are fleeing through the gates in search of solid land and dry.

Let the bishop start to run,
and Lady Webbe prepare
to meet her fate, for porters wait
at kitchens everywhere,
piling their carts with sweetmeats, devil's cake and angel's food,
and one large pie, all ordered by the city's great and good.

III. The Feast

Water, water swift and black
is rising in the maze.
Liquidity that mocks the sea,
the proverb here betrays.
How many vows are coming due, what plans for good or ill
can surely be completed now that water runs uphill?

Every gutter that permits
pollution to disperse
amongst the drains, this tide constrains
to function in reverse!
But what alarms from ship and shore? What panic in the streets?
The harbour is deserted for tonight, the city eats.

Lanterns cluster over boards
laden with dishes rare,
delicacy and every
manner of tempting fare!
With roast and rissole! Pastry, pie, pilaf, brochette and bake!
With tart and timbale, candy, choux, ice-cream, compote and cake!

Some bear fondant rebuses;
others a floured sign,
icing of blue or crimson hue;
aromas not divine
alert the wary to the risk such items may contain,
unless the cook is so disposed to leave the poisoned plain.

All the people passing by
and taking in the show,
of golden drape and flaming crepe:
you may be sure they know.

The Master

Some dishes sicken, others kill, all are aware and none
are forced to gamble with their lives but always, it is done!

Wealthy sorts may keep a fast
and sternly tell their spawn
who sob and sigh, what virtues lie
in pleasure once forgone.
But see the scarecrow leading skinny children down the street,
swallowing fast, then telling them which dish is safe to eat!

See women with bellies big
and others pale and thin,
grasping at meat and milk, to eat
and ease the ache within.
The beggars, sailors, prostitutes; all those who are denied
their daily needs can scarcely now their hunger override.

Watch young couples carefully
applying every test,
not just to cull the edible
but what will keep the best!
The old who have decided after years of poverty
that if they are to die, for once, they'll taste of luxury!

Not all those who eat are poor:
no, some are merely young;
these run the tracks in noisy packs,
sharing the risk among;
the bored alongside those who seek to season their delight
with weird hallucinations and the fantasy of flight.

What of the almonds atop?
What means this apple core?
A man was seen to shake and lean
but he was drunk, for sure!
The revel buzzes with surmise, with laughter, shriek and call,
and rumour that the Webbe display contains no taint at all.

****

Round and down, the bishop runs,
avoiding all his flock,
keeping to shadow like he had
intent to pick a lock.
The burning hate that guides his steps, surer than eyes or ears,
now flickers like a lantern as the sound of water nears.

What does he intend to do
once they are in his sight?
Should he not call a constable
or wait until it's light
before his family facing, for the first time in long years,
setting aside the cataclysmic aspect of his fears?

His is the judgement of God
of course, but failing that,
he is a man alone with an
overambitious hat!
Upon the threshold of the maze he halts to contemplate
the shape of his dilemma, and then sees it is too late.

Water, water wide and chill
comes pouring up the street,
erasing all below the wall
to darkness so complete,
and lapping at the heels of an unreally-sorted crew,
whose hunching backs and glaring faces he could swear he knew.

A giant of a woman
there piggybacks another,
who shrieks and rides, raking her sides
until she grumbles: "Mother!
I may be sane but if you don't stop doing that, I swear,
I'll put you onto Father: then we'll see how you both fare!"

"Show respect!" commands the man
staggering at her side.

"Had you not lost your sight the cost
 had been a fair divide!"
In horror, then, the bishop sees the font of all his fears,
the gape of sockets underneath whichever face appears.

Seeking only now to flee,
 he finds his path is barred
by sort of man as clearly can
 press such an issue hard,
who looks him over doubtfully, before demanding halt.
"You'd better bring the oracle to see what I have caught!"

"Cousin," the blind monster calls,
"just take his eyes and go!
 I swear this flood is seeking blood
 though why, I do not know.
 Wulf answered every aspect, as the master did dictate!"
But then the mounted madwoman approaches, crying:"Wait!"

"My eyes cannot be deceived –
 this fellow is our son!
 His stockings found, we thought he drowned,
 but this is he or none!"
"'Tis true!" the bishop stammers. "There is quite a story owed –
 how nice to see you!" Whereupon Lucia shucks her load.

"My brother still is living?"
 she cries. "I see he is!
 And so you planned your freedom and
 abandoned me to this!"
He does not answer as the blind man reaches for his face:
the oracle inveigles him into a close embrace.

There was once a mother who
 held him and cooed his name;
 and is it still impossible
 this creature is the same?

Both of the sorcerers exchange a queer, unseeing look
of wonder as his father says: "Perhaps we were mistook."

"One who has returned," she says,
"after an absence long."
"And who chooses," Father muses,
"to judge our actions wrong.
Do you think?" "It might well explain," she mutters. "Either way,
I don't see we lose anything by making him to pay!"

She takes hold about his legs:
he grips him by the throat,
and both propel him to the swell
and swelter of the moat!
The cousin seizes emeralds, then gives a mighty shove:
Lucia's shriek of protest is all that remains above.

The fetid substance closing
as he descends beneath,
coagulates, displaying traits
of fingernails and teeth!
He struggles as they breach his nose, his mouth and either ear,
but finds to his intense surprise he can both breathe and hear.

"What is this? What is it now?
Not him! Not him at all!"
The voices seethe, shiver and grieve:
"So let the city fall!
Let not one stone remain above, let all below decay,
but let it be my chosen spouse within my arms shall stay!"

"Sweet Virgin," the bishop prays,
"thy humble servant I,
O pardon me in thy mercy
and do not let me die!"
The waters press into his each and every orifice,
to susurrate: "If you serve me, then tell me where he is!"

It seems to the bishop that,
if Heaven's holy maid
is this morass of silt and gas,
his is a faith betrayed.
But still a pragmatist at heart, and fearing the below
more than the wrath of any god, he says, "I think I know."

He will trust to Lady Webbe
in *that*; and if he lies
it's only one more thing he's done
in order he may rise!
The water churns; he rides it like a native guttersnipe,
and only hopes he does not end inside a narrow pipe.

****

True enough that Lady Webbe
is used to such dismay;
often abhorred or else ignored,
though never in this way!
She's fighting for her soul encircled by a hue and cry
whose sole concern is why they should not venture on the pie.

"Tonight we make sacrifice,"
she says, "to those below.
If I am bound beneath the ground
there's something I would know.
Your name eluded me no matter what resort I tried.
Pray grant to me that knowledge now, and how it was you died."

Her answer comes shimmering
like mirage over sands,
and it's a blessing she can guess
the epoch where she stands,
for madness might well seize the mind that so abruptly shed
its every point of reference, and plunged amongst the dead.

Over a dark hill she floats,
and under midnight skies;

their massive frames imbued with flames,
two stony icons rise
about a girl, in truth a child, arrayed in silver fur,
staring in horrified dismay at those confronting her.

A crowd of souls encircles
those princes twain of old.
All for a festival are dressed,
even the corpses cold.
With golden torc the victor stands, and grips his brother's hair
and though his eyes are bleeding, by the gods, that one is fair!

It is a wedding banquet
thrown into disarray,
with basted meat and cakes made sweet
with rosemary and bay,
with forest fruits and honey, trampled down into the mud
by such as would despoil the rose and mingle wine with blood.

That a traitor won the night
is witnessed by the skin
of roasted doe split open to
reveal weapons within!
And yet he claims the prize, for none shall ever offer more
of value than his brother's blood upon the sanctum floor.

She forbids him to proceed,
that tiny priestess queen,
with eyes defying earth for sky
and courting the unseen.
The prophecy upon her lips is muffled by his kiss.
What numinous prerogative is overthrown by this!

Think of all the countless dead
that made this hillock grow
after that child in sorrow smiled
and leapt from high to low!

The water takes her swiftly: all around the men exclaim!
But then the fairer brother casts himself into the flame.

"Thus our city is begun,
  with sacrifice awry,
  with rapine and with contraband,
  and though we sure deny
  the truth of it, still we adhere to patterns that were laid
  into the deepest stratum on the night you were betrayed."

The lady sighs: slowly now
  the square about returns.
"The truth repressed, how could you rest?
  And so your anger burns,
  relying on the empathy of those who see the past,
  to raise you up into the light. I see I am the last.

"And why should I not aid you,
  you've suffered here so long?
  Do I not feel that to reveal
  the truth is never wrong?
  Why should I not do all within my power to assist?"
"Because," a muffled voice declares, "he will be sorely missed!"

Those about to cut the pie
  scatter like startled birds;
  all appetite has taken flight
  at these surprising words!
  The pastry shudders, cracks and heaves; a mirror to the ground
  that starts to open, spreading fear into the streets around.

Now the gutters overflow
  and chimney pots are filled.
  Now hollow gargoyles swallow
  more than they ever spilled!
  Not blazing fire but water bursts from under paving riven
  in aqueous abandon, by undying passion driven.

Lady Webbe has eyes alone
for he who burns below,
who'll be restored for such reward
as only she can know.
Now reaching down, she grasps at curls a writhe with spectral flame,
as though all elements have here become one and the same.

Doctor Wulf is tenderised,
basted and lightly herbed,
but he will do what he must to
see this disaster curbed.
A carving knife to cut his bonds, a leap to clear the shelf,
only to hear the lady cry: "Now goddess, show yourself!"

"I have seen you are in truth
no more divine than I!
It seems the myth we're dealing with
our nature would deny!
Come stand before me, state your case to those you would destroy!
Explain to us why we should die for but a single boy!"

Waterlogged and wretched thing
emerging from the crack,
trailing a mess of ruined dress
smeared over with the black
ensuing from the bishop's mouth as he begins to keen:
"Oh where now, whist now: what is this? A woman, well I ween.

"I see you are of my kind,
possessor of the sight!
But queen or slave, you shall not save
my last, my one delight!
Is it your right to choose a king? Is it your choice to die?
Rather than live a slave, would you embrace the Deep, as I?"

"But what of the hundreds who
rejoin you every day?

For everyone under the sun
must fall beneath your sway."
"They die much in the way they live, and live much as they die,
and never once lift up their eyes or ask the reason why.

"Yes, 'tis true I summon them
from feasting as from fray:
all those who gain from our long pain
have dreadful debts to pay!"
The lady keeps her courage as the bishop starts to spout:
"How dare you reignite the flame I finally put out?"

"But what of the thousands who
still worship at your fane?
Is all they do to honour you,
like that man's life, in vain?"
"They fastened me inside a box and set his ashes free!
And that is how these man-priests show their reverence for me!

"For a thousand years I have
waited my wedding night,
but his own flame between us came
with but this one respite!
Beloved, oh! You did not burn when we embraced before!"
"Mistress," the doctor ventures, "your forgiveness I implore.

"The sorcerers who took me
and bound me in that bath,
cherished a plan to free your man
and then divert your wrath
by offering a substitute, perhaps the best they had.
I'd like to say I'm flattered, but now truly they are mad."

The bishop's body billows
but worse perhaps is this:
the lady's skin is blackening
from fingers up to wrist!

The orbits of an oracle hold him in fierce regard
from out a pallid visage that escaping tears have tarred.

"Woeful this and wearisome
to me, and yet I find
I know you for a warrior,
a healer good and kind.
So if my chosen one has truly turned away his face,
were it thus freely done I might accept you in his place."

"Don't you dare!" The lady gasps
"I'll let the master go!"
The doctor smiles grimly the while,
"You cannot now, I know.
If you must burn or I must drown, I will sustain the jape."
The lady screams: "Ridiculous! Why can't they both escape?"

In sudden comprehension
the doctor turns and runs.
Despite a scream like bursting steam,
into the church he comes
and seeking, like a fugitive, for sanctuary divine,
he tramples through the kneeling throng and throws open the shrine.

Pitiful the spectacle
he thus reveals to view!
The brethren's fears dissolve in tears:
it seems that no one knew
the Virgin of the seven shrouds is but a childish corpse,
and tannin-stained, and shrunken as the marsh all matter warps.

Racked by pangs unthinkable
the lady does her part:
what dances now upon that brow
and in that burning heart?
Such beauty as to sear the soul, such will as might defy
the grasp alike of love and death, so to attain the sky.

And as the master rises
unfurling flaming wings,
along the aisle in ancient style
a choir the mistress brings.
He reaches out his hand to her: the corpse begins to burn
and to the endless firmament their aspirations turn.

Once again the city heaves,
convulsing through and through;
and it will be a mystery
to all the people who
wait out the night in foodless fear, what happened to the rift,
and how the flood could leave such lack of sediment and drift.

Stands the sanctum empty now,
desolate, save the wreck
of festival and of couple
embracing neck to neck.
Though burned and scarred, approaching old: they share a truth sublime,
that those who freed the prisoners will follow them in time.

A feast of poison purified,
a dish of hate redeemed,
transcending all of sweet and gall
that's by the world esteemed.
If all that walk the planet's crust of dust and ashes eat,
'tis those who dare imagine more that find themselves replete.

The Final Offering

IV. The Finish

"Where is the master's glory
  and where the astral gate?"
The sorcerer can but infer
  that they are come too late!
"Lucia, this is all your fault! We are condemned to earth!
  I'll pop your eyes and drown you like you should have been at birth!"

"Father, you will drop your hand,
  and use a civil tone!
The lord knows I could watch you die
  on that account alone!
But what is this? My brother drowned where all the road is paved?
  Oh, stand aside and let me work: perhaps he may be saved!"

Pummelling the bishop's back
  and breathing fit for two,
the cook persists until he twists,
  and starts to shake and spew.
A stinking flood bursts from his lips, a liquid rancid, thick,
  but then he whispers weakly: "Oh my lord, I do feel sick.

"Sister, my dear Lucia,
  is that your face I see?
Oh please don't let our father get
  his fingers into me!"
"Hush, my dear lamb, I'm with you now and though I share your pain,
  that horror cannot touch us here and never will again.

"Cousin, come and help him up:
  bring Mother here as well.
I have in mind that we must find
  another place to dwell.

Those gemstones you are carrying will surely ease our way;
but Father must remain behind, his murders to repay."

And as the pure light of dawn
anoints the highest spire,
the chime of bells a new age tells,
with little blood or fire.
A city with a history, whose heroes it condemns
but which may yet accept the change that has been wrought by them.

Day Sleep

Index of Titles

Bat's Boudoir, The	29
Battle Bride, The	18
Cat's Cortège, The	32
Day Cars	60
Deshayes Cradle Song	12
Exorcism	51
Fare, The	81
Fear, The	69
Feast, The	93
Finish, The	107
Flower Maid, The	16
Grandchild, The	46
Herbal Tea	9
Hymn	63
Kite, The	20
Land of Dreams Gone Bad, The	3
Mary	7
My Guest	62
Night Cars	5
Rat's Repast, The	36
Sculptor, The	53
Sleep of Reason (concluded), The	65
Sleep of Reason (interrupted), The	49
Soldier's Return, The	23
Torturer's Confession, The	13
Traveller, The	43
Vespers	59
Virgins and Martyrs	56

INDEX OF FIRST LINES

A maiden dwelt within this glade,	16
As proudly sound the martial drums,	18
Blest be he who shuts my eyes	59
Come into the graveyard, Mary,	7
Do you know what they did to him?	63
From those first monoliths raised	81
Goblins sleep in the roots of herbs,	9
Hark the bells in the bright air!	69
I am a master of exacting craft.	13
I conjure thee, oh spectre of belief,	51
It's Saturday and the traffic is horrendous,	60
It's time that you were moving on, the afternoon is past,	43
Its brick	46
She goes home tonight.	20
The door's too thin, the noise gets in;	53
The light is running from the sky	62
The parties have all run on too long	3
The ride was hard and howling dark	23
The white tower rose	65
There is a bell	49
They hang from the thorn there,	56
Water, water swift and black	93
What does it take to kill a mouse?	12
When sleep wraps the house in a blanket of wool	5
"Where is the master's glory	107

Glossary

amphibrach. In poetic metre, a metrical foot of three syllables, consisting of one accented syllable flanked by two unaccented syllables (*A Reader's Guide to Literary Terms*, 1970).

amphimac. In poetic metre, a metrical foot of three syllables, consisting of one unaccented syllable flanked by two accented syllables (*Reader's Guide*).

chiroptera. From Chiropteran: any member of the order Chiroptera, with membraned limbs serving as wings, including bats and flying foxes (*Concise Oxford*); bats have long been associated with witchcraft, black magic and darkness; they are a symbol of ghosts, death and disease; vampires are said to be able to shape shift into bats (Wikipedia article on the Bat).

chorist'. Short, by poetic license, for chorister; chorister: a singer in a choir (*Merriam-Webster's Collegiate Dictionary*, 2003).

datura. Any poisonous plant of the genus Datura (*Concise Oxford*); belongs to the classic "witches' weeds," such as deadly nightshade, henbane and mandrake; contains toxic hallucinogens, and can cause delirious states and death; an essential ingredient of love potions and witches' brews (Wikipedia article on Datura based on Preissel's *Brugmansia and Datura: Angel's Trumpets and Thorn Apples*, 2002).

djert. (d-rt) Word known from a very early period in Ancient Egypt and used continuously throughout, referring both to professional mourners and the bird of prey; see *Dancing for Hathor: Women in Ancient Egypt*, by Carolyn Graves-Brown (UK: Continuum, 2010).

Note: Most meanings are taken from the *Concise Oxford Dictionary* (Eighth edition, 1992) unless otherwise marked. Where extra notes are employed in the same entry *Concise Oxford* is cited to differentiate.

enspelled. Use of poetic license; similar to ensorcell: to bewitch, enchant (*Mirriam-Webster's*).

ergot. A psychotropic mold that grows on rye, noted for its hallucinogenic properties when ingested (from Wikipedia article "Dancing Plague").

felis. The cat genus (*The New Imperial Reference Dictionary*, [1900]); cats feature widely in legends, myths, folklore and fairy tales and were venerated in ancient Egypt; black cats were associated with witchcraft and black magic in Medieval times (from Wikipedia article, "List of fictional cats and other felines"; http://rulingcatsanddogs.com/cat-legends; and *New Larousse Encyclopedia of Mythology*, London: Hamlyn, 1968).

gawd. Same as gaud, a piece of finery (*Imperial Dictionary*).

habeas corpus. A writ requiring a person to be brought before a judge or court (*Concise Oxford*); literally means "you have the body" in Latin.

hartshorn. An ammonious substance from the horns of a hart (*Concise Oxford*); used in medieval times in food preparation and in "smelling salts" (from http://www.foodtimeline.org/foodcookies.html).

hinderance. Prevention, obstacle (*Imperial Dictionary*); same as hindrance.

ichor. (In Greek mythology) fluid flowing like blood in the veins of the gods.

in nomine patris. In the name of the father; Latin term [in prayers the p is usually capitalised] (online: http://www.latin-dictionary.org/In_nomine_patris_et_filii_et_spiritus_santi).

jennet. A small Spanish horse.

ka. The name given by ancient Egyptians to a presiding or second spirit supposed to be present in a human being or statue (*Macquarie Dictionary*, Fourth edition, 2005).

lairy. From lair, (Scot.) mud, to mire, adj. lairy (*Chambers Twentieth Century Dictionary*, 1966); meant here to imply a strong, damp scent of earth.

lex talionis. The principle or law of retaliation that a punishment inflicted should correspond in degree and kind to the offense of the wrongdoer, as an eye for an eye, a tooth for a tooth; Latin term (online: http://dictionary.reference.com/browse/lex+talionis).

macle. A twin crystal; a dark spot in a mineral.

masquers. Variant of masker: a person who wears a mask (*Merriam-Webster's*).

murine. Of or like a mouse or mice.

must. Grape-juice before fermentation is complete.

nog. A small block or peg of wood; a snag or a stump on a tree.

pretensing. Poetic license for verb, to pretend.

recherché. Carefully sought out; rare or exotic.

scrying. From scry: divine by crystal-gazing.

susurrate. With some poetic license; word comes from susurrus and susurration, pertaining to "a sound of whispering or rustling."

torc. A necklace of twisted metal.

vervain. Any of various herbaceous plants of the genus *Verbena*, esp. *V. officinalis* with small blue, white, or purple flowers; traditionally connected with witchcraft due to its nervine qualities.

wight. A person (*Concise Oxford*); a Middle English word for living being or creature, especially human being.

SELECTED BIBLIOGRAPHY OF KYLA LEE WARD
as of September 2011

Novels

Prismatic. Co-authored with David Carroll, and Evangelos Paliatseas, as "Edwina Grey." Sth Melb, Vic.: Lothian Books, 2006. Won 2007 Aurealis Award for Best Horror Novel. Shortlisted for the 2007 Ditmar Award for Best Novel.

Short Fiction

"The Feast." In *Aurealis* #24 (1999).
"The Boneyard." Online at gothic.net (Sept 2001).
"Poison." In *Passing Strange: A New Anthology of Australian Speculative Fiction*. Edited by Bill Congreve. Parramatta, NSW: MirrorDanse Books, 2002.
"Sakoku." In *Agog! Fantastic Fiction: 29 Tales of Fantasy, Imagination and Wonder*. Edited by Cat Sparks. Wollongong, NSW: Agog! Press, 2002.
"Kijin Tea." In *Agog! Terrific Tales: New Australian Speculative Fiction*. Edited by Cat Sparks. Wollongong, NSW: Agog! Press, 2003. Shortlisted for the 2003 Aurealis Award for best short horror and the 2003 Ditmar Award for best short story.
"The Last Communication of Dr. Kent Lawson, Truffle Hunter." Online at vilewatchers.com (Jan 2005).
"The Oracle of Brick and Bone." In *Borderlands* #5 (2005).
"The Bat's Boudoir." In *Shadowed Realms* #9 (2006). Shortlisted for the 2007 Ditmar Award for best short story. Reprinted in *Australian Dark Fantasy and Horror*. Edited by Angela Challis. Woodvale, Western Aust.: Brimstone Press, 2007.
"A Tour of the City of Assassins." In *Ticon* #4 (Jan 2009).
"Cursebreaker: The Welsh Widow and the Wandering Wooer." In *Scary*

Kisses. Edited by Liz Gryb. [Bentley], Western Aust.: Ticonderoga Publications, 2010.

"Erina Hearn and the Gods of Death." In *Macabre: A Journey Into Australia's Worst Fears*. Edited by Angela Challis and Dr. Marty Young. Woodvale: Western Aust.: Brimstone Press, 2010.

Poetry

"Mary." In *Bloodsongs* #3 (1994). Honourable Mention in *The Year's Best Fantasy and Horror:* 8, edited by Ellen Datlow and Terri Windling (1995). Reprinted online at *Gothic.net* (Feb 2002).

"Herbal Tea." In *Bloodsongs* #6 (1995). Reprinted online at *Gothic.net* (Mar 2002).

"Night Cars." In *Abaddon* #2 (1999).

"Exorcism." In *Midnight Echo* #5 (2011).

"The Land of Dreams Gone Bad." In *Midnight Echo* #5 (2011).

Artwork

"Rootibos." Illustration to "Herbal Tea." In *Bloodsongs* #6 (Spring 1995).

"Adoration." Cover for *Epiphanies of Blood: Tales of Desperation and Thirst* by Bill Congreve. Parramatta, NSW: MirrorDanse Books, 1998.

"The Musical Is Dead." Illustration for "Relish" by David Carroll. In *Southern Blood*. Edited by Bill Congreve. Sandglass Books, 2003.

"Scapegoat." Illustration for "The Purgatory Machine" by Richard Harland. In *Borderlands* #2 (Aug 2003).

"Spirals." In *Fables and Reflections* #7 (Apr 2005).

"But What About The Symbolic Dimension Of My Actions?" Cartoon. For *Newswrite* #163 (Dec–Jan 2007), NSW Writer's Centre.

"Or Would I Achieve Greater Impact By Suggestion?" Cartoon. For *Newswrite* #163 (Dec–Jan 2007), NSW Writer's Centre.

"True Love? Or Does The Book Just Need More Sex?" Cartoon. For *Newswrite* #163 (Dec–Jan 2007), NSW Writer's Centre.

As Editor

Tabula Rasa: A History of Horror, Issues 1–7 (1994–1995). With David Carroll.

Articles

"Gaming Freeform." In *Australian Realms* #17 (1994).
"Australia." In *The BFI Companion to Horror*. Edited by Kim Newman. London: Cassell, 1996.
"Scaring the Children." In *Viewpoint: On Books For Young Adults* 5, no. 1 (1997). Full version printed in *Bloodsongs* #8 (1997).
"Playing the Classics." In *Black Gate* #4 (2002).
"Castle, Sweet Castle." Online at d20weekly.com (9 Oct 2002).
"Get Lost." In *Dragon* #326 (Dec 2004).
"Tomb Raider." In *Dragon* #327 (Jan 2005).
"The Petit Tarrasque and Other Monsters." In *Dragon* #329 (Mar 2005).
"Australian Gargoyles." In *Art Monthly Australia* #200 (Jun 2007).
"Coffin Culture." In *Black: Australian Dark Culture* #3 (Nov 2008).
"Dark Humour in *Revelation of the Daleks*." With David Carroll, and Kate Orman. In *Time, Unincorporated 2: The Doctor Who Fanzine Archives* (Vol. 2: Writings on the Classic Series). Edited by Graeme Burk and Robert Smith. Mad Norwegian Press, 2010.
"Symbolism." With David Carroll, and Kate Orman. In *Time, Unincorporated 2: The Doctor Who Fanzine Archives* (Vol. 2: Writings on the Classic Series). Edited by Graeme Burk and Robert Smith. Mad Norwegian Press, 2010.
"Dungeons and Deadlines." In *QW Magazine* #207 (May 2011).

Role-Playing Games (RPGs)

Mystical Places. Web resource for the Unisystem. First instalment (2001). Second instalment (2001). Third instalment, "The Scalper": in *Eden Studio Presents* #3 (2009). Eden Games Studio.

Co-authored *The Demon Storyteller's Guide*. White Wolf Games Studio (2002).

"Suffer the Children." In *Fear to Tread*. White Wolf Games Studio (2003).

Contributor to *The Demon Players' Guide*. White Wolf Games Studio (2003).

Contributor to *Damned and Deceived: The Book of Thralls*. White Wolf Games Studio (2003).

Contributor to *Demon: The Earthbound*. White Wolf Games Studio (2003).

Contributor to *Time of Judgment*. White Wolf Games Studio (2004).

"The Court of Chimera." In *Eden Studio Presents #3* (2009).

"Dominion." In *Pyramid Magazine #3/10* (Aug 2009).

Scripts

Bad Reception. Directed by Andrew Orman. 4TOD Productions (2008). Screened at A Night Of Horror 2009, and the Vampire Film Festival 2009. 6 min 54 sec.

Chocolate Curses, "a comedy in dubious taste." Directed by Steve Hopley. Played as part of the Season II program of the Theatre of Blood, April–July 2010. 20 minutes.

The Land of Bad Dreams by Kyla Lee Ward.
(September 2011; rpt, February 2016)
ISBN: 978-0-9804625-7-9 (illustrated paperback) $14.50AU

OTHER PUBLICATIONS FROM P'REA PRESS

Richard L. Tierney: A Bibliographical Checklist by Charles Lovecraft.
(February 2008)
ISBN: 978-0-9804625-0-0 (paperback) $6AU

Spores from Sharnoth and Other Madnesses by Leigh Blackmore.
(September 2008; rev. rpt, August 2010, May 2013, February 2016)
ISBN: 978-0-9804625-2-4 (paperback) $14.50AU

Emperors of Dreams: Some Notes on Weird Poetry by S. T. Joshi.
(November 2008)
ISBN: 978-0-9804625-3-1 (paperback) $14AU
ISBN: 978-0-9804625-4-8 (hardcover, out of print)

Savage Menace and Other Poems of Horror by Richard L. Tierney.
(April 2010)
ISBN: 978-0-9804625-5-5 (illustrated numbered hardcover) $30AU
ISBN: 978-0-9804625-6-2 (illustrated ebook) $10AU

Avatars of Wizardry by George Sterling, Clark Ashton Smith, et al.
(November 2012; rpt, February 2016)
ISBN: 978-0-9804625-8-6 (illustrated paperback) $14.50AU
ISBN: 978-0-9804625-9-3 (illustrated ebook) $10AU

Dark Energies by Ann K. Schwader.
(August 2015; rpt, August 2015; February 2016)
ISBN: 978-0-9943901-0-3 (illustrated hardcover) $26AU
ISBN: 978-0-9804625-1-7 (illustrated paperback) $14.50AU
ISBN: 978-0-9943901-1-0 (illustrated ebook) $10AU

P'REA PRESS

Publishes weird and fantastic poetry and non-fiction
c/– 34 Osborne Road, Lane Cove, NSW, Australia 2066
Website: www.preapress.com
Email: DannyL58@hotmail.com

CPSIA information can be obtained
at www.ICGtesting.com
Printed in the USA
FFHW020120071119
56001484-61861FF